G. R. ELTON was born in 1921 and educated in Prague and at Rydal School before obtaining a London University External B.A. in 1943, and a Ph.D. in 1949. He served in the army during the war, and then held the post of assistant in history at Glasgow University from 1948 to 1949. From 1949 to 1953 he was an assistant lecturer at Cambridge, becoming a lecturer in 1953. In 1954 he became a Fellow of Clare College, Cambridge, and was made a Fellow of the British Academy in 1967. Professor Elton has held visiting lectureships at the Universities of Boulder and Pittsburgh in the United States, and also at Belfast and Oxford. He presently holds the post of Professor of English Constitutional History at Cambridge. He edited the second volume of the New Cambridge Modern History, and among his best-known works are *The Tudor Revolution in Government* (1953), *England Under the Tudors* (1955), *Tudor Constitution* (1960), *Policy and Police: the enforcement of the Reformation in the age of Thomas Cromwell* (1972) and *Reform and Renewal* (1973). Professor Elton is the series editor for the Fontana Library of English History, and has written *Reformation Europe* for the Fontana History of Europe.

D1430435

G. R. ELTON

THE PRACTICE
OF HISTORY

COLLINS·FONTANA
In Association with Sydney University Press

First published by Sydney University Press 1967
First issued in Fontana 1969
Seventh Impression April 1976

© G. R. Elton, 1967

Made and printed in Great Britain by
William Collins Sons & Co Ltd Glasgow

CONTENTS

PREFACE

There have never been more historians at work in the world than there are to-day. Among these masses of active scholars, many have presumably at some time reflected upon their craft, but only few have published their thoughts. Though in this the many may have been wise, the practical result has been that, with the exception of manuals instructing in techniques of research, most books on history have been written by philosophers analysing historical thinking, by sociologists and historiographers analysing historians, and by the occasional historian concerned to justify his activity as a social utility. This contribution seeks to avoid the last, ignores the second, and cannot pretend to emulate the first. It embodies an assumption that the study and writing of history are justified in themselves, and reflects a suspicion that a philosophic concern with such problems as the reality of historical knowledge or the nature of historical thought only hinders the practice of history. When I read discussions of how historians think, how they can claim to describe that which no longer exists, or whether historical fact has an existence independent of the thinker about facts, I marvel at the ingenuity of the writers, for usually they are men who have never apparently themselves tried to do the work, to see the manifestly surviving evidence of past fact and event, or to practise critical judgment on the materials of history

rather than the minds of historians.[1] Though I have
looked at a good deal that has been written around
these matters, I have made no effort at an exhaustive
or comprehensive investigation. What I have tried
to do is to set down experience—my experience in the
study, writing and teaching of history. This is a manifesto rather than a treatise, more an explanation of one
working historian's faith and practice than a systematic
analysis with a series of proved conclusions. I know,
of course, that my experience has been limited and
that my examples, for instance, will seem to have been
chosen from a narrow sector of history. However, I have
endeavoured to remember that there is a great deal
more history than I know about, that there are
methods of studying it which I have not had occasion
to practise, and that there never is any single road to
success.

I know that what I have to say may at times appear
offensive, and I can only hope to be believed if I say
that I have tried to reserve my criticisms for men whose
eminence I recognize and that I have thought only of
the issues involved. It would be quite improper to reduce one's personal responsibility for a manifesto by
calling in the friendly support or help of others, and
I shall not do so. But I must record my thanks to those
who over the years have listened patiently and critically
to my diatribes; and I want to express my gratitude to

---

[1] I do not mean to deny that there are some sensible books on these
subjects, as e.g. W. H. Walsh, *An Introduction to the Philosophy of History*
(London, 1951); P. Gardiner, *The Nature of Historical Explanation*
(Oxford, 1952); W. B. Gallie, *Philosophy and the Historical Understanding*
(London, 1964). Every new number of *History and Theory* is liable to
contain yet another article struggling to give history a philosophic basis,
and some of them are interesting. But they do not, I fear, advance the
writing of history.

the Sydney University Press, and especially to Mr Michael Turnbull who not only suggested this book to me but from first to last gave me encouragement and excellent advice. Authors do not often feel well disposed towards editors; this one does.

Clare College, Cambridge   G.R.E.

December 1966

For this edition I have corrected a few errors of fact and added an index; otherwise, the text remains un-altered.

November 1968

I

Purpose

1 The Present Debate

The future is dark, the present burdensome; only the past, dead and finished, bears contemplation. Those who look upon it have survived it: they are its product and its victors. No wonder, therefore, that men concern themselves with history. The desire to know what went before, the desire to understand the passage down time, these are common human attributes. Yet one must distinguish. Though creation myths and cosmogonies testify to this universal desire to give meaning to the past, not all civilizations have been equally concerned to know and write human history as it really was. Modern civilization is peculiar rather than ordinary in that it rests upon the two intellectual pillars of natural science and analytical history. Theology and philosophy can both claim to have commanded the minds of men for longer stretches of time and over larger areas than these characteristic thought systems of the twentieth century, thought systems which significantly enough, came jointly to dominance in the seventeenth. Their triumph, now universal, has itself been the outcome of an historical situation, for the political and technological advantages which gave Europe the victory in the struggle of civilizations brought to the top a complex of societies whose thinking had been influenced by the longest traditions of a real concern with the past. There is something markedly a-historical about the attitudes embedded, for instance, in the classic minds of India and China, and any history of historiography must needs concentrate on the Hellenic and Judaic roots of one major intellectual tree. No other primitive sacred writings are so grimly chronological and historical as is the Old Testament, with its express record of God at work in the fates of generations succeeding each other in time; and the Christian descendant stands alone among the religions in deriving its authority from an historical event. On the other hand, the systematic study of human affairs, past and present, began with the Greeks. Some sort of history has been studied and written everywhere, from the chronicles of Egypt and Peru to the myths of Eskimos and Polynesians, but only in the civilization which looks back to the Jews and Greeks was history ever a main concern, a teacher for the future, a basis of religion, an aid in explaining the existence and purpose of man. And even there, its present-day standing is of quite recent origin.

The study of history as a properly developed discipline is really quite young, younger by far than that of medicine or law, philosophy or theology, even of the natural sciences. *Ante Agamemnona*—before Niebuhr and Ranke—the great men did exist, but the mass of historians was neither large nor remarkable. Herodotus may have been the father of history, but for a good many centuries the child he begot was to enjoy but a restricted and intermittent life. Thucydides, Polybius, Livy, Sallust and Tacitus—great names but, for some 600 years, not a terribly impressive tally; and it is not without significance that the one historian among the ancients for whom no one has a bad word seems to be Asinius Pollio of whose writings nothing survives. Medieval chroniclers occasionally rose above their annals

to reflect and explicate,[1] and by now we have all heard
of Ibn Khaldoun. Renaissance history—Bruni, Machia-
velli, Guicciardini—has received more applause than
readership, and there are those who would call Francis
Bacon an historian, on the strength of that quite
untrustworthy piece of brilliant journalism, his *Life of
Henry VII*. It was, in fact, the seventeenth century that
took the first purposeful steps towards serious historical
study. Mabillon and the Bollandists founded the science
of the criticism of sources; in England, Spelman, Selden
and Brady wrote something recognizable to modern
professionals; Wanley and Maddox investigated the past
from its true relics; a bit later, the Göttingen school
weighed in, too, and transferred the initiative to
Germany.[2] Resting on the advance made by the humanists, men like these gave history the right to regard itself
as an independent form of enquiry, seeking its own
answers to its own problems, and following its own canons
of proof and purpose. They looked for causes, for a
connecting chain in the seemingly meaningless sequence
of events, and if they could be crudely mechanical they
also taught that there is secular sense to be made of past,
present and future.

However, despite these often remarkable achievements,
the scientific, ordered, systematic study of history really
began only in the nineteenth century, because only
then did historians absorb the lessons of the antiquarians

[1] V. H. Galbraith, *Historical Research in Medieval England*
(Creighton Lecture: London, 1951).

[2] M. D. Knowles, *Great Historical Enterprises* (Edinburgh, 1963);
F. Smith Fussner, *The Historical Revolution* (London, 1962); J.
G. A. Pocock, *The Ancient Constitution and the Feudal Law*
(Cambridge, 1957); D. C. Douglas, *English Scholars 1660-1730*
(London, 1939); L. Fox, ed., *English Historical Scholarship in
the 16th and 17th Centuries* (London, 1956); H. Butterfield, *Man
on his Past* (Cambridge, 1955).

and develop to the full the techniques which enabled them to answer the common charge that their reconstruction of the past was just a tale, amusing and instructive enough, but without any rigour, certainty or standard of truth. Dr Johnson, though aware that historical facts might be known, could not trust 'the characters we find in history, unless when they are drawn by those who knew the persons' : and Catherine Morland could not understand her boredom with history when 'a great deal of it must be invention . . . and invention is what delights me in other books'. Fifty years later, history was being written on the foundation of systematic research. The results would still have seemed morally uninteresting to Samuel Johnson and would still have bored Miss Morland, but for different reasons. The inventions and fancies, the character sketches, were being replaced by tested certainties, and open questions by problems.

There is therefore a very real sense in which good modern historians are superior to greater minds and abler men who in earlier ages concerned themselves with history. There is no arrogance in this : they are so because they have been allowed to become better scholars. To the literary mind, the great English historians may be Clarendon, Gibbon and Macaulay, even though hardly anyone reads them any longer and their readability is their main claim to fame. Surely, they are worth reading and wrote splendid books, but they wrote in the prehistoric age and therefore lacked the opportunities which we markedly lesser men enjoy. To the historian, the great English historians are Maitland and Namier, even though they never wrote long histories : for which reason it must hastily be added that one's admiration for them is not based on, is rather tempered by, this one deficiency. It is not just knowledge or the ability to understand motive which makes the true historians; on those grounds, no doubt, that elderly trinity surpasses many even of the good moderns. The difference lies in the different attitude and purpose brought to the study by a mind trained in history as a scientific and intellectual approach.

It need, then, cause no surprise that with that one civilization's general dominance in matters of standards and beliefs the study of history should in the last 300 years have assumed the appearance of a major intellectual industry. The amount of history that is written to-day (quite apart from the amount that, though studied, never gets written), and the number of people engaged in various ways in the investigation of the past, should frighten or exhilarate, according to temperament and the phase of the moon. Moreover, like every good service industry, history has something for everybody. Individual craftsmen, working for the few, exist side by side with mass-production factories supplying the needs of the many. All the signs are of health. The university departments are full of students; and teachers of history, laid end to end, might even reach from premise to conclusion. Publishers fall over each other in the rush for historians: even academic historians have at last realized that they own a marketable commodity and need not be quite so awed by the publisher's cheque-book. The series multiply. The whole business is beginning to show the marks of a run-away boom : hectic production leading to dilution of quality, price inflation, and ever more insistent warnings from the apprehensive that all good things must come to an end. Indeed, there are signs that we may be reaching that crisis of confidence which can precipitate a slump. At every turn one encounters visceral investigation; the working historian's life is increasingly beset by the specialists in moral exhortation and the prophets of doom.

In some sense, this unsystematic debate is itself a sign of life, though it cannot be denied that life, as usual, involves occasional touches of disease or malformation. Nor is there a great deal that is new in all these doubts and warnings. A good many critics demand that historians should leave the shelter of their muniment rooms and libraries in order to play their part in creating a general intellectual climate; but do they know that they are only repeating the arguments of Voltaire and the eighteenth-century philosophical historians against the antiquarians whose researches they despised?[3] Those who preach the virtues of statistical, sociological or other 'scientific' methods are only reviving, after an interval so short as not quite to excuse their ignorance of the fact, the weary argument whether history is an art or science.[4] Because its materials are necessarily partial, and the products emerging from individual minds more partial still, history always has posed and always will pose the sort of problems which give rise to dispute, acrimony, and the writing of hostile reviews. Why, at the very beginning of our science stands the prototype of all these arguments: history had barely begun when Thucydides attacked the methods and purposes of Herodotus. Debates among historians are

---

[3] Cf. A. D. Momigliano, *Studies in Historiography* (London, 1966), 1ff. It may be unkind to remember that the claims of those philosophic historians collapsed when they were found to be sadly wanting in scholarship.

[4] Whether history is an art or a science is a dead issue. It is both. But it has always been an art; the addition of science, which is the work of the last 150 years, has turned it into something new, something appropriate to the highest abilities of the human reason.

coeval with the writing of history, and like the heresies of Christianity all the possible positions were worked out quite early, to be repeated in resounding counterpoint through ages of controversy.

Above all, historians have always wondered just why they do this thing—why they study history. It may be true that a concern with the past is a widely found human characteristic, but that does not dispose of the question. It only puts it one stage back: why should people be interested in the past, and especially why should they be sufficiently interested either to devote an intellectual existence to it or to support the lives of those who do? The question why society should wish to nourish historians leads to its corollary: what should historians do to justify their existence to their society? The simple answer that to study and write history is a pleasant occupation, that it satisfies the practitioners and does no harm to anyone else, is not only too obviously narrow and selfish but may not even be true. Historical writings can do harm; they have done so; and any thoughtful historian must at times ask himself whether he has a purpose beyond his own satisfaction.

The questions may be eternal; the answers tend to go in waves of fashion, cannoning off each other in often predictable reactions to the predominant theory of the moment. Since historians are naturally given to sharpness of tongue, the debate is likely to look savage to the outsider: it is not only in intellectual ascendancy that historical studies prove themselves to have supplanted medieval theology. Nevertheless, a little bit of perspective can fairly be demanded of men who claim to be concerned with the development of things and ideas through time. Thus when we are told, by an historian now in his early thirties, that in the first half of the present century English historians had 'temporarily lost their bearings' because the political and constitutional pre-occupations proper when Britain ruled the world had ceased to be valid while nothing else had taken their place,[5] we should point out to him, gently, that he has merely failed to consider the question in a proper historical light. The many good historians whom he thus relegates to confusion and intellectual poverty did not, it is true, happen to hold certain beliefs that are fashionable now. They did not necessarily suppose that only social analysis has value in the study of history, and they did not, on the whole, suppose that they must justify their labours by reference to some non-intellectual effect upon society. But this does not mean that they were not possessed of principles and creeds as definite, and as potentially limiting, as those proclaimed by their critics. The first half of this century was dominated among English historians by a conviction that the principles of respectable historiography could be reduced to one main precept : to study history for its own sake. Though this austere rule could and did produce a fair amount of narrow tedium, it also resulted in some most remarkable monuments of the historian's craft. It is, so far, by no means clear that those who react against it are likely to write history anything like so well founded, so careful in its pursuit of the truth, or so uninfluenced by preconceived ideas and ready-made answers. Their chances of doing so are at present hard to judge because after quite a few years of manifestoes and occasional

---

[5] Keith Thomas in *Times Literary Supplement*, 7 April 1966, 275. The whole of that article, and indeed of the issue of which it formed part (called 'New Ways in History'), is shot through with an engaging arrogance and historically invalid assertions. But it raises serious questions, and I shall recur to it throughout this chapter.

learned articles they have notched up a still surprisingly small amount of identifiable achievement.

Neither the fact that the debates can become otiose, nor their zeal in so often simply echoing the points made in the past, need, however, lead one to suppose that the proper cure is silence. The debates are necessary and, even at their most jejune, not totally without worth. Like all those who practise the concrete sciences, historians are always in danger of contenting themselves with the daily grind. An age of debate is an age of stock-taking; it leads to a necessary reformulation of purpose and principle; and though the answers are never going to be really new they may yet throw new light and accumulate new insights which will assist in the real purpose, in the study and writing of history. The recent and continuing outburst of self-doubt, lavish criticism, and prescription of panaceas has been accompanied by much superficial shouting, much whoring after false gods, much petulant assertion of doubtful tastes and standards. But these defects do not rob it of its fundamental justification : it attacks a complacency which could become mindless. However, it does seem to me that the time has come to restate some of the truths of practice and experience, to rescue history from its candid friends, and to remind the historical world that there is work to be done rather than to be called for, that that work must be carried out in a cage set by certain inescapable conditions, and that bright ideas, however seemingly new, are not everything.

In this chapter I shall concern myself with three main issues. It is first of all necessary to ask once again whether history has an identity independent of other forms of study : does history exist as an intellectual pursuit, can it claim to possess its own rules and principles, or is it merely a hold-all for various other 'social sciences'?

Secondly, arising from this, its proper relation to cognate disciplines must be looked at. Lastly I shall offer my answer to the question : why should we study history?

2 *Autonomy*

The study of history comprehends everything that men have said, thought, done or suffered. That much is commonplace, but also not quite true; some reservations have to be made. In the first place, not all the past is recoverable, and the study of history is necessarily confined to that part of it of which evidence either survives or can be reconstructed in the mind. That is to say, while history may commonly be thought of as the whole of mankind's past life, it is in truth equal only to the surviving past. Historical study is not the study of the past but the study of present traces of the past; if men have said, thought, done or suffered anything of which nothing any longer exists, those things are as though they had never been. The crucial element is the present evidence, not the fact of past existence; and questions for whose answer no material exists are strictly non-questions. True, this is a less limiting reservation than may be thought because the surviving traces of the past are not confined to material survivals; evidence can to some extent be discovered where it appeared not to exist, and the historian's techniques at times enable him to reconstruct that which is lost from that which is still around. Yet the limitation remains important, especially in practice. Lively minds of little knowledge like to charge historians with asking the wrong questions or with treating uninteresting problems. The history of princes and politics, of war and diplomacy, is often called dull and insufficient; why do we not hear more about 'ordinary people', the lives of the poor, the whole of 'society'? The charge can be true, but only if in fact the evidence for the study of such problems exists. If it does not, they have no place on the historian's table. The past is over and done with: it cannot be relived. It can be reconstructed—seen and understood again—only if it has left present matter behind.

Secondly, the definition given is in a way too wide because history is not the only form of enquiry which deals with man's past life. All the so-called social sciences—archaeology, anthropology, economics, social psychology, sociology—attend to man, and all of them can concern themselves with his past as well as his present. This is quite apart from the fact that strictly they can never consider the present: at the moment of being considered it becomes the past. These sciences are clearly autonomous; they deal in methods, questions and results which are peculiar to themselves. Is history autonomous in this sense—is it indeed a specialized form of enquiry or merely an attitude of mind employable in these other sciences? Sociologists, in particular, are capable of asserting such a claim; I once heard one of them say that the study of the past is superfluous because a true understanding of the present, arrived at by sociological analysis, enables one to extrapolate and explain the past. (He did not appear to be joking.) However, the arrogance to which sociologists are prone does not preclude the possibility that occasionally they may arrive at some not entirely obvious truth not discoverable by historical enquiry alone. We must therefore ask how history differs from other studies of man if that difference is not found in its concern with the past. The answer lies in three habits peculiar to history: its concern with events, its concern with change, and its concern with the particular.

History deals in events, not states; it investigates things that happen and not things that are. As against this, archaeology, for instance, can only uncover and describe states, conditions and circumstances symptomatic of a particular way of life; it is unable to handle the fact of life, which is movement. Archaeological states follow jerkily one upon another, without description or explanation of the movement, and it matters nothing whether the transformation is gradual (undatable), as it usually is, or catastrophic. When the archaeologist attempts to incorporate events in his analysis, he either has to confine himself to the bare fact essentially equal to the description of a state ('this site was destroyed by fire') or to resort to historical statements that do not arise from his archaeological evidence and methods, and which, if he is studying a period for which no historical account is possible, may have to be purely imaginary. Anthropology or sociology, on the other hand, may well display interest in the event—in a circumcision ceremony or a wedding, in the building of a school or the formation of an opinion—but this will not be for the sake of the event but for the sake of extracting static conclusions from moving elements. The historian may well interest himself in the state of things, the condition of society, the principles underlying a system of government or a system of thought. But if he is to understand historically and practise historical writing, he will have to think of such analyses as steps in a chain of events, as matters explanatory of a sequence of happenings. He will have to concentrate on understanding change, which is the essential content of historical analysis and description. History treats fundamentally of the transformation of things (people, institutions, ideas, and so on) from one state into another, and the event is its concern as well as

its instrument. To suppose that causal
are the main content of history is an e
form but a particular case of the general p...
history deals in movement from state *a* to state *b*. If *a*
can be said to have caused *b* the relationship happens to
be causal; but it is none the less properly historical
if *a* and *b* are linked by coincidence, coexistence, or
mere temporal sequence, all relations very often encountered in history, however less intellectually satisfying
they may be.

As for history's preoccupation with the particular, that
must be seen in its proper light. It is often asserted that
the special distinction of the historical method is to
treat the fact or event as unique. But frequent assertion
does not create truth, and this statement is not true. No
historian really treats all facts as unique; he treats
them as particular. He cannot—no one can—deal in the
unique fact, because facts and events require reference to
common experience, to conventional frameworks, to (in
short) the general before they acquire meaning. The
unique event is a freak and a frustration; if it is really
unique—can never recur in meaning or implication—it
lacks every measurable dimension and cannot be assessed. But to the historian, facts and events (and people)
must be individual and particular : *like* other entities
of a similar kind, but never entirely identical with them.
That is to say, they are to be treated as peculiar to themselves and not as indistinguishable statistical units or
elements in an equation; but they are linked and rendered
comprehensible by kinship, by common possessions, by
universal qualities present in differing proportions and
arrangements. The historical event is like the modern
physicist's atom, composed of analysable and repeatable
ingredients but so composed as to be itself complex and
in a measure unpredictable; and not like Newton's

om or Leibniz's monad, a basic and identical unit
of matter. This is what is meant by the false assertion
that the historical fact is unique, and one can see that
for practical purposes the error can seem very like the
truth. But the distinction is vital because reasoned
analysis of the complexities of the past and avoidance of
the standardizing mistakes of the social sciences are
not possible unless the true definition is grasped.

We can now rephrase the earlier definition of history.
It is concerned with all those human sayings, thoughts,
deeds and sufferings which occurred in the past and
have left present deposit; and it deals with them from
the point of view of happening, change, and the particular. Since no other treatment of man's experience answers
to this definition, the autonomy of history—its right to
be distinguished from cognate sciences—is established.

3 Kinds

Within this comprehensive definition of history, we
ought perhaps to distinguish different kinds. The writing
of history and the understanding of the past take many
forms, and no one, probably, who has ever thought
about these matters, can avoid believing in some hierarchy among them. Thucydides, for instance, opened
the story of debates among historians by questioning the
possibility of any history except contemporary history.
To him this was the inescapable conclusion to be drawn
from the fact which has been mentioned: that history
is only equal to its evidence. He thought that only
personal experience and observation could guarantee
knowledge and accuracy. 2500 years later, that argument
is still sufficiently alive for an American historian to
ask the ironical question whether the past should concern

the historian at all.[6] In giving a warning against an excessive preoccupation with the contemporary, he adopted a position probably more common to-day than that of Thucydides, if only because developing techniques have given us a better control over the evidence for more distant ages and left us aware of the exceptional difficulties involved in discovering and assimilating the evidence for our own times. One also meets the opinion that special virtues adhere to this or that period of history, as it might be the European middle ages, or the nineteenth century, or some great age of Cathay. Such arguments may sometimes be valid when the purpose of study is in question; some well-worked or well-documented pieces of history may have advantages in teaching others, as some obscure or little known bits may assist the historian in marking out his claim to recognition. But no argument exists which successfully establishes a hierarchy of worth among historical periods or regions as such.

Yet though we need no longer think in those terms, we are still inclined to make distinctions supposedly based on differences of intellectual content. To some commentators, no history that does not tell a story deserves the name at all, while others object to anything but pure analysis as below the highest aspirations of the historian. Most people do not admit to such clear-cut prejudices, but the prejudices are there all the same. In truth, historians, like other people, tend to judge their world from their own experiences and practice, and it is distressing to see how narrow in their sympathies even eminent men can be. E. H. Carr, for instance, has spent a great part of his life writing the history of Russia in

[6] Charles E. Nowell, 'Has the Past a Place in History?', *Journal of Modern History*, xxiv (1952), 331ff.

the twentieth century; fundamentally, he has worked on a narrative account in very recent history. But does this entitle him to judge the state of our knowledge of fifth-century Greece from the fifty-year-old memories of a Cambridge undergraduate, or to write off a great part of medieval studies because he mistakenly thinks that the bulk of evidence surviving from the middle ages was produced by monastic chroniclers?[7] These are errors based on ignorance; another derives from his limited understanding of the historian's range of tasks. 'I have no patience,' he says, 'with the fashion . . . of pretending that Mommsen's greatness rests not on his *History of Rome* but on his corpus of inscriptions and his work on Roman constitutional law; this is to reduce history to the level of compilation.'[8] If the last sentence were true one might no doubt agree with him. But his exasperated complaint shows no sign that he grasps what Mommsen achieved when he laid the solid foundations of Latin epigraphy, or of the kind of organizing and analysing genius required in the writing of the three large volumes of the *Staatsrecht*. The sheer learning and expository skill displayed in these works exemplify historical insight and achievement of the highest order; to recognize this, which need not induce one to deprecate the sweep and grandeur of the *History of Rome*, should, in the working historian, call forth an awed admiration for greatness in his own line of work. By comparison, narrative history might almost be called easy, though Mommsen's practice of it, even if intellectually less mountainous than those other works, remains marvellously impressive in itself. But both types of writing are history.

The reason for Mr Carr's somewhat philistine judg-

[7] E. H. Carr, *What is History?* (Penguin edition, 1964), 13-14, 149.
[8] *Ibid.* 37.

ment is obvious enough : he himself has specialized in the production of narrative history on the grand scale. Historians naturally praise in their fellows those enterprises and distinctions which come closest to their own mode of thought and work. It is difficult to appreciate anything that one does not know from personal experience, easy to lapse in catholic sympathy. And this is the more understandable because too universal a sympathy, too ready an acceptance of all treatments of history, would constitute an abdication of the judgment which all historians must, as a duty, preserve. Occasional grumpy disapproval is much to be preferred to that general and tepid approval which pervades, for instance, most professional reviewing of historical books in America. The motives may be creditable (not to slay the defenceless) or very dubious (not to call down similar treatment upon oneself), but in any case a real duty is neglected when no standards are set for the intellectual and artistic treatment of serious historical problems. Sympathy for a variety of concerns and manners of approach does not preclude the existence of some severe discrimination in the judgment.

However, the more obvious and more common danger is that exemplified by Mr Carr : to write off certain forms of historical study and to reserve approval for those to which one happens to incline oneself. Behind such harsh judgments lies the multifariousness of history itself. Since the whole of history—the whole of a person, a period, or a problem—can never be got between the covers of one book, some means of rendering the material manageable must be found. The commonest is to adhere to the notoriously artificial divisions into which the study of the past breaks up at the approach of a teaching syllabus or an examination system. We write political history or economic history, constitutional or administrative history, history of ideas or history of science. J. H. Hexter has called this 'tunnel history' and has castigated it with his own brand of engaging savagery.[9] That he has much right on his side cannot be denied. Tunnels do circumscribe the vision. But what is one to do? To transfer the universality of life on to paper, or even to comprehend it in the mind, is rarely possible, and without a main line of thought nothing results except the jumble which in fact is nearest to the common experience of life. This would be neither art, nor understanding, nor use. Issues and problems demand some sort of tunnel for their clarification; the past must be sorted into 'aspects' to become not only manageable but meaningful. There is really nothing wrong with thinking in tunnels, provided one remembers that there is earth above and around the tunnel, and that the shape and direction of the tunnel are governed by the constitution of the substance about it. 'Aspects' are just that : not separate entities, but forms extracted from the mass with the tool provided by the method of approach selected. All good historical writing is universal history in the sense that it remembers the universal while dealing with part of it.

There are, therefore, no ways of dealing with history which are *intrinsically* superior to others. Political history —the analysis and description of the way in which men have conducted affairs—is not necessarily more jejune than social history, the analysis and description of the arrangements by which they have lived together in ordered groups. The writer on wars and armies need not feel inferior to the student of markets, price fluctuations and methods of production. Administrative history concentrates on the manner in which institutions and instruments of government are organized and work;

[9] *Reappraisals in History* (London, 1961), 194ff.

constitutional history, which concerns itself with the principles and conflicts embodied in the development of governmental organization, is not by that token any more distinguished. In particular, the historian of thought and ideas, secular or religious, need not think (as he is inclined to) that he is somehow more elevated or significant than he who wrestles with the intricacies of law courts or strives to understand the problems involved in the edition of charters. In these matters there are no hierarchies, and mutual respect is the only proper attitude.

This does not mean that there are no distinctions to be made, but only that the distinctions do not depend on the dominant interest or the main line chosen. The differences to which the critical mind should address itself lie solely in the manner of execution. They are not confined to the degree of art displayed, to competence in explanation or skill in description. The writing of history requires powers not universally available, but the name of historian need not always be denied to the man who cannot write well. What matters are the differences shown in the intellectual treatment of the questions asked. And here the fundamental distinction is that between the amateur and the professional. This is not always an easy distinction to make, for it is not identical with that between men who earn their living by the study of history and those who engage in it by the side of other occupations. The distinction I have in mind rests between the man who has learned his job and the man who, sometimes with touches of genius, comes to it in a happy spirit of untrained enterprise : crudely, the distinction between those who think that research means reading a lot of books and those who have grasped that research means assimilating into oneself the various and often very tiresome relics of the past. Examples of both are found inside as well as outside the academic profession.

The hallmark of the amateur is a failure of instinctive understanding. This expresses itself most clearly in a readiness to see the exceptional in the commonplace and to find the unusual ordinary. The amateur shows a tendency to find the past, or parts of it, quaint; the professional is totally incapable of this. On the other hand, the professional, truly understanding an age from the inside—living with its attitudes and prejudices—can also judge it; refusal to judge is quite as amateurish a characteristic as willingness to judge by the wrong, because anachronistic, standards. By all these criteria, Lord Acton was an amateur, and so he was, a prince of amateurs. Very wide reading and self-consciously deep thinking may have attended him; but he was for ever expressing distress or surprise at some turn in the story, was alternately censorious and uncomprehending, suspected conspiracies and deep plots everywhere. In short, he lived in history as a stranger, a visitor from Mars. The professional lives in it as a contemporary, though a contemporary equipped with immunity, hindsight and arrogant superiority—a visitor from the Inquisition. How is such professionalism created? G. M. Young once offered celebrated advice : read in a period until you hear its people speak. But this is amateurishness of a drastic kind because it is superficially professional. Who ever knew or understood people just because he heard them speak? The truth is that one must read them, study their creations and think about them until one knows what they are going to say next.

I do not mean to deny that what I have called amateur history can be very good, not only entertaining but useful and stimulating. Still less do I mean to doubt that professional history can be very bad, sterile and stultifying in the extreme. But the emotional criterion, which measures the response evoked by the historian, is a partial guide and provides no firm standard. The criterion I have offered here has about it a quality of precision. The best amateur history, however entertaining, cannot enlarge the understanding or deepen the participation because it is written from outside, through a veil woven out of strangeness and wonderment. At its best it achieves sympathy and romantic love, but it cannot penetrate to fundamental explanation; at its common bad, it is sentimental, ignorant, and an insult to the intelligence. That really fine amateur historian, G. M. Trevelyan, achieved both.

The purpose and ambition of professional history is to understand a given problem from the inside. This may well involve tedium, pettiness and pedantry, the main faults of the professional. He lacks the amateur's saving grace, for he is not doing the thing just for the love of the thing and cannot rescue himself from depression by romance and sentiment. He is struggling, sometimes grimly, with the often repulsive reality of life, and if he is a petty man or a pedant he will soon convince the reader of that. But even at his worst he cannot fail to add to learning, understanding and knowledge; he contributes truth. Thus, good or bad, he feeds the mind, while the amateur satisfies the senses. In so far as historical study is an intellectual enterprise—and that is its highest form—the professional has it every time. He is doing a job and producing results; the amateur is having fun. But there is no need to be puritanical about this. The good professional, too, has a good deal of fun in doing the job; the sad thing is to read so many professional historians who convey nothing but an agony of the spirit.

Professionalism is the product of a certain aptitude

worked upon by a specific course of training. Good historians may be born, but true historians are made. The principles and details of their training shall be touched on later; here I am concerned with the mark which that training sets upon the practitioner. In the first place, he knows his evidence. He knows the range of it, how it came into existence, what people or institutions produced it, what it can tell and what can never be got from it. In consequence he knows the 'right' questions—those capable of being answered and those that lead to further questions. His instinctive familiarity with the evidence results in a useful and necessary sense which extends his range beyond the strict confines of the evidence; even his guesses bear the stamp of truth because they fit the reality of the situation. Sir John Neale used frequently to speak of his 'hunches', and he played them very successfully. This professional hunch is based on an expert understanding of what can, what must, have happened; more than a guess, it is in the nature of an inspired forecast which often leads to the discovery of evidence supporting it. Those unaware of how the professional historian's mind works are liable to suppose that this amounts to no more than the convenient adjusting of the evidence to the preconceived idea; but though this can happen, it is rare with the properly trained professional. When the answer comes out as expected, it is because the expectation rested on profound knowledge, a knowledge which beyond the facts comprehends setting, atmosphere, possibility, probability—all those tenuous compounds in the lives of men which we call the spirit of an age. This is not to say that historians are allowed to use 'the spirit of the age' to explain things in the absence of evidence; only the amateur falls back on such vapours as the *Zeitgeist* or a national character. The professional uses his real awareness of what is 'right' in a given context in order to fight his way through to an explanation grounded on evidence. It is a tool of selection and divination, not an end to the process of reasoning and discovery. This solid kind of familiarity lies behind everything that is professional about historians; from it flows the ability to understand an age in its own terms, to judge it by the criteria appropriate to itself, to avoid the error—the 'whig' error—of looking only for what has significance in a later age, and to distinguish between the commonplace and the exceptional.

This distinction between the amateur and the professional deserves so much emphasis because it is really fundamental. Both kinds of historian require other capacities, such as ability to judge evidence, ability to construct an argument or a narrative, ability to write. The final product will owe much to these further qualities which may be found equally present or absent among amateurs and professionals alike. But the difference in the foundations will always show through. However much we may prefer to read the amusing amateur rather than the tedious professional (admitting that the adjectives may well at times be changed round), we shall trust the second when we really want to know.

It may be objected that in confining distinctions between historians to this single point I have ignored too much, and in particular that I have wilfully misunderstood the distinction between history and compilation which Mr Carr made in his comment on Mommsen. Is all work in history to be judged only by the amateur or professional status of the historian? Are there no basic differences in the kind of work attempted? Is the editing of a chronicle on a level with the writing of an imaginative narrative, the analysis of an institution equal to the unravelling of social relationships? Answers to these questions will depend on the ground upon which the enquirer takes his stand. This present enquiry turns on the intellectual worth of historical studies, and from that point of view there are no differences that do not arise from the historian's basic attitude to his materials. An honest professional job of any kind deserves equal respect; an honest amateur job merits a different and less searching appraisal. We hear to-day a good deal about the absurdities of minute research, especially in Ph.D. theses. An eminent scientist has condemned those who crawl upon the frontiers of knowledge with a magnifying glass. But what is wrong with taking a magnifying glass to the frontiers of knowledge? Surely that is precisely where it is needed. Perhaps one may want some man at times to stand up, gaze around, and look beyond; but unless they have taken an active part in the painful mapping of the advancing frontier, the visionaries are nothing but a menace. I have no patience (to quote Mr Carr) with the common attitude of contempt for the young student who labours on what may seem a narrow or petty subject and attempts to master the techniques of study which it can teach, though I would agree that the mature scholar who still seems to be at that stage of interest raises one's doubts and hackles. Except for examiners, who are paid for it, no one needs to read Ph.D. dissertations, but those who flatter themselves that they can make a valid distinction between what is important and what merely superfluous in such enterprises, elevate personal taste to the level of a critical standard. Judging thus, they have no answer to those who sniff at their own splendid and ranging edifices because they think them unsound or (this can happen) tedious. Research work of this journeyman kind deserves to be judged by the only tests it seeks to satisfy: is it honest and exhaustive, has it asked questions that are right and adequate in the context of the problem, has it found reasonable answers, does it prove the author to have learned his trade? And much the same point applies beyond the stage of the Ph.D. dissertation. Good and bad work can be done at all stages of historical enterprise; and the standard of quality to apply must be defined as intellectual honesty and intellectual penetration within the compass of the problem investigated.

The historian's ability and knowledge are as much called upon in the editing of a text as they are in writing the history of the Russian Revolution, though the result will attract different sorts of readers. There are also matters of degree and intensity to be allowed for, but none of kind. Mommsen displayed genius in his *History of Rome*; but he also displayed genius, as well as greater skill and greater knowledge, in his *Römisches Staatsrecht*. In the hand of some Professor X, neither would no doubt have been successful, though both would have been as legitimate—and as properly called history— as they were in Mommsen's hands. Naturally no one denies that historians differ in quality of mind and personal capacity. Mr A's excellence and Mr B's stupidity may mean that Mr A writes history and Mr B something else. But the point must be judged by reference to the manner in which each discharged his task, not on the grounds that Mr A's great gifts enabled him to write a history of China while Mr B confined himself to the editing of a medieval chronicle. Compilation does exist, but only rarely does it not require, embody and reflect a learned understanding of history, quite as much as it provides means for enlarging that understanding. One need not go so high as Mommsen's *Corpus Inscriptionum*: let Mr Carr try his hand at compiling trade statistics for English cloth exports in the sixteenth century and see how far he can get without a full use of a true professional equipment. And in applying that equipment to the establishing and recording of reliable figures, he would be writing *history*.

This last example makes plain that the argument is in danger of becoming absurd. Common sense forbids one accepting the view that no distinction can be made in essence between the compiling of trade statistics and the treatise on the history of trade which rests on such statistics. Yet if my premise be allowed—that judgment must depend on the question whether the work flows from adequate knowledge and is honestly executed— the deduction follows; and I certainly stand by my premise to the extent of regarding it as legitimate and important. But I agree that other premises can be found, premises which others may treat as more mean- ingful and fruitful, though I should hesitate to do so. In particular, Mr Carr, and others who think like him, would judge by the purpose which a piece of historical writing is meant to serve. They wish to see history justified from outside itself, and to rank its products by standards derived from that desire. It is often felt that the subject cannot claim the status, either as a science or as a useful art, which belongs to other disciplines that deal with man : it should therefore both learn from them and approximate to them. Before we can consider the purpose of studying history, we must therefore look at its relations with the mentors and rivals that have been set over against it.

4 Rivals

Autonomy is not the same thing as exclusiveness or self- sufficiency. There are things to be learned. Archaeology can assist history by recovering evidence and thus help to recreate the historical event which archaeology itself is incapable of analysing or describing; inserted into the framework of history, it can also contribute expansions of the time-scale (as in the history of ancient Egypt) or add areas of historical study by making historians ask new questions, as in the reconstruction of Roman military organization or the exploration of medieval farming habits. This asking of new questions is the chief lesson which sociologists have taught to historians who have learned to consider the 'structural' problems of society—the analysis of social hierarchies, relationship of classes, mobility among them, the importance of common assumptions and social myths. Anthropology has opened historians' eyes to the significance of social habits, the mixture of the universal and relative which goes to make up the ways in which people accustom themselves to living in groups. The obvious importance of economics and social psychology—the manner in which they enable the historian to construct wholes out of patchy evidence by teaching the general rules governing the behaviour of forces, crowds and individuals—needs no stressing. Since men's experience in the past, as at all times, was clearly influenced by what happened inside them, between them, and around them, every form of enquiry which touches on these circumstances is of use to the historian; and this may include not only the sciences of man but also the sciences of nature. Provided the instruction received is turned to historical use, provided it is used to consider and explain change in the human past, these borrowings can be nothing but fruitful.

All this is so patent that every generation produces a loud demand for more borrowing, more humility on the historian's part, more worship at the shrines of practitioners whose self-confidence springs from their claim to be scientists. They, we understand, produce certainty, where the historian is at best able to produce dialectical argument. The prophets of each generation rather touchingly believe themselves to be the first innovators, and in old age they are often found among the most bitter opponents of the next wave of prophecy. However, enthusiasm is not perhaps the best state of mind in which to contemplate questions of method and procedure. The German historicism of the nineteenth century, now so much under a cloud, took its first inspiration from two sources : the textual criticism of the philologist, and the mechanics of physical science. In consequence it was inclined to a rather mechanical view of history; it dealt too readily in plain chains of cause and effect. The attack upon it certainly came in part because the progress of historical research itself called in question many of its confident conclusions, but once again too many historians looked to other studies for instruction. Towards the end of the last century, the dominant sciences of physics and philology were replaced by biology, anthropology and sociology, with the result that history became both subtler and less certain, more relativist and more aware of the variety of circumstances that make up any given situation. Despite the conviction of some English scholars to-day that they are the first to bring the social sciences into the working habits of English historians, that trinity of mentors has remained virtually unchanged since; all that has happened is that new and often more rigorous techniques used by them have come to the attention of the historian looking for 'new methods'.

There are two chief reasons for these iterated invitations to use tools borrowed from elsewhere. One is the natural desire of young men to find new things in fields much tilled by their predecessors. Some minds most readily formulate new questions under the influence of some theory that has caught their attention. The much advertised social questions—structure, habits and ambitions—have in fact been asked by historians since Herodotus, which is not to deny that we have refined our techniques and occasionally enlarged our interests, often under the stimulus of some other discipline. But the notion that only direct borrowing from very recent sociology or anthropology has drawn historians' attention to 'such matters as harvests and food-supply, epidemics, and medicine, the age of marriage and the size of families',[10] is an illusion quickly dispelled by a little study of earlier writers. The famous antiquarians of the seventeenth and eighteenth centuries were mainly interested in these and similar questions, and if they may now be despised for their preoccupation with collecting data and their failure to produce analytical conclusions, it is not at all clear that their present-day successors have advanced all that much further in this respect.

Too careful an ear cocked for the pronouncements of non-historians is liable to produce disconcerting results. Anthropology and sociology do not stand still; there are probably few disciplines in which the differences among the learned are more ineradicable and more ferocious. The humble historian may only too readily find himself listening to the wrong party or catch on to views already abandoned by the *avant garde*. Thus we are still enjoined on occasions to call in Freud when studying people in history, at the very time when psychologists are poised for a mass-flight from Freud.[11]

10 Keith Thomas, *T.L.S.* 1966, 276.
11 I cannot feel that the much-praised Freudian effort of E. H. Erikson, *Young Man Luther: A Study in Psychoanalysis and History* (London, 1959), contributes anything of value to an

The anthropology which influences the most modern historians is still too often at the Malinowski and Margaret Murray stage.[12] Marxist sociology, long since overtaken by more accurate and more subtle analyses, remains powerful among historians, and its influence is by no means confined to those aware of it; fragments of class-struggle theories and economic determinism are found curiously embedded in the work of scholars who at the conscious level do not believe in them but need them to satisfy their wish to be thought 'deep'. 'Lonely crowd' and 'affluent society' theories are swallowed trustingly by the alert historian who then proves less able to disgorge them again than are his sociological instructors themselves. Admittedly, the historian is not always ill-advised to be so backward; in the social sciences fashions come and go with disconcerting speed, and by sticking to his point on the wheel the historian may as quickly come to the top of the turn again as by clambering about the wheel while it revolves. Nevertheless, one is justified in asking those propagandists for more social science in history just which kind, school or doctrine they are recommending. My own experience of these debates includes several occasions on which the most fervent advocates of the use of sociology by historians were told by the priests of their golden calf that clearly they neither knew what sociology was nor had any understanding of its recent developments.

---

understanding of either Luther or his age. In so far as it has been responsible for John Osborne's play, it may even need condemnation.

[12] Mr Christopher Hill accepts 'the validity of the main thesis of Dr Margaret Murray's *The Witch-Cult in Western Europe*', though he boggles 'at some of her illustrations of it' (*Society and Puritanism in Pre-Revolutionary England*, London, 1964, 187, n. 4). For this he is gently but justly criticized by Professor G. E. Aylmer (*Eng. Hist. Rev.* lxxxi, 1966, 785-6).

However, the desire to open up new lines of enquiry (even when they are not all that new) is a reputable one, and if this endeavour finds stimulus in the methods and conclusions of others it should by all means seek it there.[18] The other main reason for this constant looking over the fence is rather more dangerous in its effects, for it stems from historians' dissatisfaction with one of the essences of their calling, which is that it can never on its own terms establish scientific laws concerning the history of mankind. To use terms current among modern philosophers, history is 'idiographic', that is, it particularizes, and not 'nomothetic', that is, designed to establish general laws. An idiographic science can, it seems to me, become nomothetic only if the particulars it studies become numerous enough for statistical generalization from them to be valid, and here history is likely to be forever handicapped by the smallness of the sample. Even allowing four generations to a century, we have information about only some two hundred generations, and for the vast majority of them our information is extremely patchy. I doubt if any statistician would find this an adequate sample from which to extract the sort of general laws (the fates of civilizations, tidal movements of nations, and that sort of thing) which some historians wish to discover. Of course, the historian should generalize—that is, express larger conclusions based on his particulars. But to some types of mind that activity lacks reality unless the limited generalizations proper to the historian ('in certain circumstances men are liable to do this or that') turn into laws ('in stated conditions, the following results will predictably ensue').

[18] The time may just about be upon us when literature and language are once more promoted to the task of inspiration— even if we have nowadays to call them semantics. The signs are multiplying and the prospect is attractive.

Hence the laws of economic determinism, or the biologically based determinism of Spengler and Toynbee, with their powerful attraction for those to whom the tentative and particularizing 'idiography' of history is emotionally unsatisfying. The kind of science which history can be has nothing to do with 'nomothetic orientation'—does not demand the creation of a framework of laws—for such a framework is always essentially *a priori*; but that is not to deny it scientific status in its own terms, namely the function of a descriptive and analytical science, producing a series of experimental truths.[14]

Few practising historians would probably nowadays fall victim to the search for laws; the experience of research is enough to cure such ambitions. But a good many hanker after a certainty and precision which they believe to be proper to a science and which, in their view, traditional historical methods lack. They go to sociology and the like not only for inspiration but especially for method and can speak with hope of an 'age of the historical factory' with its cooperative and organized scholarship calling upon arithmetic for aid.[15] I am less frightened by the thought of cooperative research or 'quantification' than unimpressed, so far, by its results, and I believe that these supposedly sophisticated innovators are guilty of a little naïvety. They cry for the sun of reason and learning in ways familiar down the ages, but they have mistaken the heavenly body before their eyes : in fact they are crying for the moon. There are three good reasons for this. Historical materials

[14] For a useful discussion of these and similar points see Louis O. Mink, 'The Autonomy of Historical Understanding', *History and Theory*, v. 24ff.

[15] Thomas, *T.L.S.* 1966, 276. To the best of my knowledge, Mr Thomas, a fellow of St John's College, Oxford, and the author of some excellent articles, has never worked even within sight of one of these 'factories'.

are nearly always unsuitable for the kind of studies envisaged; the comparative method conceals within itself a self-destructive error; and sociological results in history are as a rule remarkably jejune.

Sociological enquiry is distinguished by its object and its method, the object being the analysis of social relationships and the method the counting of heads in categories. History may fairly concern itself with past social relationships, and the historian may often be well advised to count heads; but it should always be recognized that, since history must analyse and relate the story of past change and must concern itself with particular people as well as categories, historical studies derived from sociological influence can never be more than a small part of the whole enterprise. In addition, they are the part least well provided for by the evidence the past has left behind. These scientific investigations of family, class, occupations, mobility and all the rest happen to excite present-day interest and began systematically little more than a century ago; since before that time interest in them was rare and unscientific, it is useless to expect to find really exhaustive materials from which now to satisfy it. Every historian encounters immense difficulties as soon as he tries to collect worth while statistics for any problem before the year 1800 or so. Too often, the figures just do not exist, and even a trained acquaintance with statistical techniques can never quite get over the problems set by samples that are not so much random as obscurely weighted both by the accident of survival and, more importantly, by the lack of concern felt for them by those who preserved them for reasons quite different from those which now motivate their study. The endeavour is not, of course, entirely hopeless, and the results of enquiry may be interesting; the trouble is that they can never be any more certain than results arrived at without these aids in method. Demographic studies, in particular, have very important uses and can sometimes rest on reasonably reliable figures; but I have never yet seen a work of this kind which did not firmly proclaim the insufficiencies of the evidence, warn against excessive reliance on its statistical tables, and then proceed to treat the explicitly doubtful conclusions as safe ground for further confident inference. Historical evidence only very rarely resolves any sizeable question for good, and it is unfortunate if particular tricks of method lead either their exponents or the reader to suppose that certainty has been at last created.

A recent and most impressive product of this socio-logical school of history, Lawrence Stone's *Crisis of the Aristocracy 1558-1641* (Oxford, 1965), provides some useful lessons. The vast work contains many sections in which the fashionable method plays no part, and it may be only a conventional historian's prejudice that I find these more conventional chapters the most persuasive in the book. However, the author himself clearly loves best the massive evidence of his tables on which he rests his striking major conclusions. The aristocracy, he argues, underwent a general economic decline which so reduced its social influence that on the eve of the English Civil War it had ceased to be an effective agent for hierarchic government in the members of the realm. This important generalization depends entirely on the reliability of the statistics, and very slight shifts in percentages would demolish the structure. Only one of Mr Stone's re-viewers has, so far, had the necessary knowledge to reconsider both the materials from which the tables are constructed and the tables themselves, and he felt com-pelled to call some crucial figures in question. The acrimonious correspondence which followed showed beyond doubt that there was quite enough uncertainty about them to permit a range of inference stretching from a mild improvement in position to a rather drastic deterioration.[16] I myself have methodological doubts concerning the figures produced in the chapter on education. Not only do I find some of the 'constructed' totals, put in where the evidence fails, unconvincing, but I wonder how one takes the step from mere figures of matriculation or even graduation to an assessment of educational standards. Questions of this sort soon rattle the bones of table-making, carefully locked in private drawers.

The trouble is that such things as the wealth of the aristocracy have to be calculated from figures very hard to systematize. Before the figures can even be added up and the percentages worked out, all sorts of questions have to be solved: who comes within the categories studied, how is wealth defined (for instance, the problem of debts owed and owing), what kind of wealth can be measured, what is the real meaning of the figures in the record, how far can statistical method fill gaps in a series, what can be done about changing values of money, and a great many more. Mr Stone, of course, considers questions of this kind, but he himself very rarely claims to have arrived at certainty in his answers. Even if agreement on all these questions were possible, and there is little enough sign of this, the real meaning of the further inferences would remain troubled by the tentative uncertainty—the roughness of the estimates conceded by Mr Stone—which the nature of the evidence imposes. Yet the landed wealth of the seventeenth-century aristocracy is relatively well documented, by comparison, for instance, with the profits or losses of

---

[16] *T.L.S.* 1966, 285f., 347, 407. The review was anonymous. But see also G. E. Aylmer in *Past and Present*, no. 32, 113ff.

court office or the familial history of the whole group; and everything about the aristocracy is well documented by comparison with other layers of society. Historians who put all their money on this kind of study and their trust in the guiding hand of sociology come to believe in certainties they have not demonstrated; they are likely to inflict many ill-established generalizations on the history books unless they show themselves more consistently aware of the deficiencies of both materials and methods than they would appear to be. There are some questions, however interesting, that cannot be answered, and attempts to force answers to them in the teeth of the historical evidence produces at best hypothesis, at worst false dogma. By all means let us have more studies of this kind, but let them be a little more modest in their claims; above all, let their proponents realize that these are neither the only nor necessarily the best ways of studying the past.

In any case, investigations on the scale attempted by Mr Stone are rare, and too many of his fellow-prophets seem content with a much more dangerous practice. They in effect accept the 'models' produced by their admired preceptors and use a form of analogical argument to apply them to history. In an earlier generation, the influence of biology, and especially of the theory of evolution, on late-nineteenth and early-twentieth century historians provided a notorious example. Here historians found a doctrine in natural science which took account of their own cherished preoccupation with change, and which seemed to make undoctrinaire sense of it. Death and decay, survival and renewal, are obvious facts of human history: it seemed reasonable to see them rationalized by the theory which explained similar events in the history of species. The result was an eruption of, or perhaps only a greater authority for, conventional metaphors speaking of youth, maturity, decline, progress, survival of the fittest, and so on. The effects have sunk into conventional thinking on history and into its vocabulary; they are very hard to eradicate. The mistake may appear obvious when it leads to the biological determinism found in Oswald Spengler's *Decline of the West*, or in the sort of history which uses theories of national or racial superiority to explain sucess and failure as part of a large plan. The evolutionary theory of history has a good deal in common with that which sees the hand of God in history; after all, evolution was thought to explain the facts of natural creation in default of the existence of a creator. Such sweeping surveys, embodying the notion that what happened was bound to happen, attract by their simplicity but are among good historians readily undermined by the habits of caution and particular study to which they are trained. Less easily detected and eradicated is the biological error *in parvo*, the sort of metaphorical explanation which, for instance, treats the English Parliament at some stage as 'mature' and thinks in terms of an earlier childhood and adolescence, as though that institution—that congregation of identifiable and always adult men—had a biological history of its own, comparable to that of the individual. (When did it reach senility?)

The devotees of anthropology are particularly prone to this kind of analogical error, as when nineteenth-century Bantus and Polynesians are called in to explain things about supposedly primitive societies of the past like pre-Columbian America or German forest tribes. Study of a more strictly historical kind at once reveals such enormous differences in circumstances and situations that the value of such comparisons—even their capacity to suggest new questions and insights—becomes very problematical. In the article already quoted several times, Mr Thomas asserts that 'Englishmen are now disposed to see analogies between their history and that of "underdeveloped" African countries in a way that Victorians could never have done.' 'The gain', he adds, 'in understanding and comparative sense is incalculable.'[17] But is it? Or rather, if it were properly calculated, would it be all gain? When some writers can treat pre-industrial England, the economically most advanced society in the Europe of its day, as though it were like tribal Africa or nineteenth-century India, understanding is destroyed, not assisted. The medieval villein of England was, unquestionably, a peasant; but this does not mean that we can learn more or better about him by studying other kinds of peasant still in existence than by un-ravelling the historical evidence (such as it is) for what his life was really like. That perfectly useful concept, feudalism, was not discredited till historians applied it undiscriminatingly to any society from Aztec Mexico to Shogun Japan in which some of its characteristics seemed to turn up. Assuredly, analogies and comparisons evoked by some other discipline can have their uses; they can reactivate a mind tired of struggling with seemingly dead or insoluble problems, and can sometimes give meaning to details of the evidence. But unless two things are remembered they are not so much dangerous as pointless: the answers must still arise from a study of the historical evidence scrutinized according to the standards of the historical method,[18] and comparisons are

[17] *T.L.S.* 1966, 276.
[18] An interesting paper by Mr Lawrence Stone on 'Social Mobility in England, 1500-1700' (*Past and Present*, no 33, 16ff.) seems to me to suffer shipwreck on this condition. He starts with a 'model' (actually quite a good one) but thereafter accommodates his discussion to that model, deducing consequences and collecting such material as helps the argument in footnotes which break the rules of historical scholarship. They are eclectic, cite whole books

usually more fruitful when they draw attention to differences rather than to likeness.

Finally, one would be more impressed by the claims made for the 'new' methods if the results proved more striking and less predictable. Too often vast engines are assembled, and blows of enormous weight are struck, only to produce an answer which is either obvious, well known, or manifestly unhelpful. In his excellent study of Charles I's civil service, Professor G. E. Aylmer, intent on reducing every problem to the certainty of established figures, provides a rather fine case in point in the section which studies the allegiance, in the Civil War, of men whose only common denominator was office under the Crown.[19] The question itself is not only legitimate but important; the treatment involves no fewer than nineteen tables in twenty-three pages. The office holders in question, not so numerous perhaps as to make percentual variations appear very large, are sliced all ways, by age, social status, length of service, distribution of property, religious affiliation, and so forth. It would indeed be interesting to know whether any of these characteristics correlate with the choice made on the outbreak of war. However, the results, expressed in properly cautious language ('considerably more likely', 'a little less likely') either show nothing of significance or underline the obvious and expected, as that older men were less likely to take up arms than younger, or that men with property in the shires controlled by the king inclined a little

---

rather than specific passages in them, and make no attempt to criticize the evidence used. This was a paper intended to be read in a discussion, and as such it is brilliant; but it would be very rash to suppose that its conclusions are soundly enough based for the confidence with which they are stated.

[19] *The King's Servants* (London, 1961), 393-416.

more to his support. The climax comes with a table which shows from a sample of twenty-three that Catholics and High Anglicans were more likely to fight for the king and Puritans for the Parliament. Perhaps such 'proof' that religious convictions had something to do with the formation of parties in the war can be useful at a time when Church and religion are no longer regarded as the major issues of the conflict; but it does seem a poor reward for so much labour.

The general desire for 'new questions' seems to suppose that the historian can get his questions in one place and then go to another where he will find the facts of the past waiting to be reconsidered in the light of ideas supplied from outside his own area of activity. It has been conceded that reading or listening to other scholars of all sorts can sometimes give the mind a new key, but the way in which these innovators wish to work leads to either silence or disaster. Unless the evidence makes the 'new' question meaningful, the in-quirer can be only honest (that is, admit that there is nothing to say) or dishonest (that is, construct himself an answer by twisting, overburdening, or even inventing the evidence). The facts known about the past are in control. However desirable it may be that we should have knowledge of past vital statistics and demographic movements, it is simply the case that for the greater part of history we shall always know very little or nothing concerning such things. Those determined to put their faith in 'sophisticated' mathematical methods and to apply 'general laws' to the pitifully meagre and very uncertain detail that historical evidence often provides for the answering of just such interesting and important questions, are either to be pitied because they will be sinking in quicksand while believing themselves to be standing on solid earth, or to be combated because they darken counsel with their errors. Sometimes methods of counting and analysing yield valuable results, but they can do so only if there exists the sort of evidence which has already inclined historians to hold the views to which the 'sophisticated' machinery gives firm foundations. This is not at all to deny the virtue of systematic study, or even the occasional virtue of IBM machines; it is, however, to assert that these points, as all others in the historian's work, achieve virtue in the light of his evidence, his historical method, and his unprejudiced hard labour.

The sociologizing historian may well retort that to replace impressionist opinion by the certainty of figures is a true advance, and I have already agreed that not every use of these methods brings either error or the commonplace. What really matters is that, obvious or unexpected, the answers carry no conviction and are not worth the time spent on them if the alternative discipline has been allowed to be master rather than servant. The historian must not go against the first conditions of his calling: his knowledge of the past is governed by the evidence of that past, and that evidence must be criticized and interpreted by the canons of historical scholarship. New methods may improve his handling of that evidence, but they can do so only if they are controlled by the historical method, which grounds detail upon evidence and generalization upon detail.[20]

[20] Professor W. O. Aydelotte, praised (e.g. by Mr Thomas) for introducing computerizing methods into the study of nineteenth-century Parliaments, has himself been more modest and much more sensible in his assessment of the interaction between history and sociology: 'A Statistical Analysis of the Parliament of 1841: Some Problems of Method', *Bulletin of the Institute of Historical Research*, xxvii (1954), 141ff.; 'Geschichte und Sozialwissenschaften', *Welt als Geschichte*, xiv (1954), 212ff.; 'Quantification in

This insistence on the hard work of specifically historical research is particulary necessary because the historian who thinks that he has found better new methods in allied disciplines too often shows an inclination to accept their conclusions without critical consideration. To give an example: economists hold that a country intent on industrializing itself needs to have an accumulation of unused capital and the means to transfer it freely from the sector which accumulates to the sector trying to expand. It was therefore long axiomatic that these things happened in eighteenth-century England, and historians wrote histories of the Industrial Revolution showing them in existence and at work. The evidence, however, shows them non-existent,[21] and it has therefore become necessary to abandon whole sections of inherited lore about the Industrial Revolution, lore which was really only assumption based on the doctrine of the theorists.

One can understand why some historians fall into this trap: the historical evidence by itself may not yield any obvious generalization, and to adopt the theories of another science may provide a coherent framework within which to arrange one's thought and description. Preconceived notions are a much greater danger to historical truth than either deficiency of evidence or error in detail, and nothing entrenches them so deep as the approval of some other form of study which seems to rest on independent thought. One could make a

---

History', *Amer. Hist. Rev.* lxxi (1966), 803ff. For a thoughtful restatement of the autonomous claims of history, linked with a convincing attack on the sociologizing tenets of the *Annales* school, see. H. Heimpel, 'Geschichte und Geschichtswissenschaft', *Vierteljahrschrift für Zeitgeschichte*, v (1957) 1ff.

[21] Cf. S. Pollard, 'Fixed Capital in the Industrial Revolution in Britain', *Journal of Economic History*, xxiv (1964), 299ff.

case for the proposition that the centuries of 'whig' historiography in England simply suffered from historians' uncalled-for willingness to let the lawyers dictate their scheme of argument. Similarly, the sociologist may provide a system of class structure or evolve theories of voting behaviour which are statistical abstracts from the multifariousness of real life. For his own purposes, these conclusions may be valid and fruitful, but no historian is entitled to assume their validity for his own period and problems: he is not entitled to know his conclusions before he has got there by specific study of the historical evidence.

When the externally obtained scheme becomes doctrine, as too often it does, it stultifies the study of history by reducing history to a repository of examples selected or distorted to buttress the scheme. The danger is greater when the scheme in fact claims to rest on a study of history, as in the 'whig' interpretation in which everything worked to the predestined end of a parliamentary constitution, or in Toynbee's system which enables its exponent even to classify as ages of peace eras manifestly filled with war.[22] Nowadays, the most complete case of this sort of disaster is that of Marxism, a universal doctrine of human history and behaviour based originally on some necessarily limited history and sociology and in its day a truly remarkable achievement of scientific insight and ill-controlled speculation. To-day, in those large parts of the world where it has become dogma, it seems finally to have prevented the fruitful progress of enquiry it once did so much to stimulate.[23]

A personal experience may illustrate this. Despite all the refinements it has undergone, Marxist historiography

[22] Cf. e.g. Pieter Geyl, *Debates with Historians* (The Hague, 1954), 119, n. 1.
[23] Cf. my remarks in *Historical Journal*, ix (1966) 388ff.

is committed to the view that in the sixteenth and seventeenth centuries Europe witnessed the triumph of a new dominant class, the bourgeoisie, with its own economic organization (capitalism) and ethos (Protestantism leading to secular liberalism). Specific study, on the other hand, impresses on the historian the fact that if any social group bettered its position and its share of political power in those centuries—and none did exclusively, anyway—it was the landed nobility, very conscious of its aristocratic status and ethos. After a little close acquaintance it becomes difficult to see the period characterized by any simple, socially-based transformation to which all dominant events, and in particular the Reformation, can be referred. In my introduction to the second volume of the *New Cambridge Modern History*, I said something to that effect and suggested that the essence of the Reformation should, after all, be sought in the realm of religion, in spiritual anguish and search. The argument is certainly open to dispute and should no doubt be discussed. But an eminent Marxist critic, a learned historian of the age, attacked my view not because the evidence seemed to him to point in another direction, but because he knew that in those years the bourgeoisie won their class war, with all the consequences that flowed therefrom in religion and the rest. For him no analysis not based on that piece of doctrine could be valid.[24] He simply did not see that the rejection, on reasoned grounds, of an interpretation cannot be answered by a reassertion, without argument or proof, of something that to him was true because it was decreed.

Doctrinaire Marxism is to the historian as special a case as doctrinaire Christianity once was, but special cases illumine the whole category to which they belong.

[24] L. Makkai, in *Acta Historica* (Budapest), 1963.

The historian is right to learn from all the disciplines which concern themselves with his own chosen subject, man through the ages. But in so learning he should walk with great care lest he fall victim to his own humility. He must beware of merely following fashion—the fashion of elevating this or that study to dominance, or the fashionable form taken at a given moment by these other studies which, since they are directed towards the extraction of laws, themselves suffer exceptionally from the vagaries of fashion. He must not adopt their methods without subordinating them to his own, and he must not use them to do what historical evidence does not permit him to do. Above all, he must not allow them to dictate his ultimate conclusion or to force upon him their so-called models.[25] Given this care, he can and should attend to them with every intention of learning. However, there is no need for this process to work in one direction only. The historian has quite as much to teach to others. He can help them to understand the importance of multiplicity where they look for single-purpose schemes, to grasp the interrelations which their specialization tends to overlook, to remember that the units in which they deal are human beings. While the historian can profit from the social scientist's precision, range of questions, and willingness to generalize, he can repay the debt by giving instruction in the rigorous analysis of evidence, sceptical thinking, and the avoidance of ill-based generalizations. Since the rashness of the social scientist, treating his theories as facts and intent on applying them in practice, constitutes one of the main dangers to which modern society lies ex-

[25] Sociologists establish 'models' which they test by supposedly empirical evidence. To an historian this seems a very dangerous procedure : far too often the model seems to dictate the selection of facts used to confirm it.

posed, the study of history may be said to serve a vital purpose when it combats the overconfidence of the men who see the world as categories and statistics, and who think in jargon.

5 Purpose

Saving the social scientist from himself (and society from the social scientist) may be a worthy reason for studying history, but not many historians are likely to regard themselves simply as specialized nursemaids and Samaritans. Some feel that they must discover that in the past which will help men to understand their present and future. The words, 'the purpose of history', have strictly two meanings: they can refer either to the purpose of the historical process, or to the purpose to be served by the historian in studying it. In practice, however, the meanings are close to each other and tend to merge. The historian who thinks that he has discerned the future towards which the past is moving conceives it his duty to instruct his readers accordingly. It becomes the purpose of his study to elucidate and demonstrate the purposes of the historical process. At the same time, it is true that even historians who do not claim to see anything significant in the way things have happened are bound to have had a purpose in mind when they entered upon their studies. No one reads or writes history in a fit of total absentmindedness, though a fair amount of history has been written by people whose minds seem in part to have been on other things.

Is there a purpose in history? Mr Carr grows very scornful at the expense of an honest man like H. A. L. Fisher, who in a famous sentence explained that he

could see none.[26] Mr Carr is surely right to denounce
the theory of the pure accident, the theory that history
is just one damn thing after another. Though in a
sense, of course, the sequence of events is just that, it
becomes history only when marshalled by the interpretative human intelligence. This is not to overlook
the importance of accidents, which do happen (though
Mr Carr would seem to suppose that they can be written
out of history), but to stress that in the understanding of
the past the accident is just another point to be explained, considered and accommodated. Accidents may
affect the course of events, but the historian, in his
analysis, must not be accident-prone. No historian, including Fisher, has in fact ever treated his subject as
though it were entirely without meaning; if he had, he
would have been unable to write. What is really at
issue is whether one may discern a larger purpose,
whether things produce effects that are continuous
and, up to a point, predictable. When Mr Carr, and
others, seek a purpose in history, they are trying to fill
the vacuum created when God was removed from history.
Even historians who hold that God reveals himself in
history would not to-day feel entitled to use him by way
of explanation, but the temperament which demands a
certain guidance from the past by way of illumination
for the future—the religious temperament—continues
to exist among historians and produce theories of the
course of history which seek this prophetic purpose.

There are in the main two ways of subordinating
history to prophecy, the circular and the linear; and
both have an ancient, respectable, and largely pre-
professional history. The first supposes that societies grow
and decay, to be replaced by others which follow much

---

[26] Carr, *What is History?*, 43, 100.

the same pattern. The other view supposes that the sum total of the past moves in a straight line of progress; though it will often allow that lapses, back-trackings and lateral movements may interrupt the main line of advance, it nevertheless insists that such a main line can be discovered and plotted. Linear theories are not necessarily optimistic, but their vocabulary (progress, advance) tends to inculcate a conviction that things not only move along a line but move towards an improvement.

To-day's best known cyclical theory is that developed by A. J. Toynbee, and it is not necessary at this date to demonstrate once again how little his vast edifice has to do with the facts of the past.[27] Linear theories are certainly commoner, and Mr Carr as well as Professor J. H. Plumb have recently entered eloquent pleas for a return to the allegedly discredited notion of progress, the notion that things get better in sum, however much the detail may get worse at times.[28] They both want historians to write to this purpose because they seem to regard it as the scholar's function not only to describe change but also to advocate it; the historian should be the prophet of an intelligent radicalism. Both abominate nostalgia about the past and wish to use history to teach men reliance on their powers to better themselves and their world. Mr Carr seems to think this right because he believes that this is the lesson of history; Dr

[27] E.g. Geyl, *Debates with Historians*, chs. 5-8. Toynbee may have contributed something useful to the study of history when he directed attention to areas and times little studied by the ordinary English historian. Even this is not altogether certain; as for his interpretative scheme and his treatment of evidence, they do nothing but harm to those who allow themselves to regard them with respect.

[28] Carr, *What is History?*, ch. 5; J. H. Plumb, ed., *Crisis in the Humanities* (Harmondsworth, 1964), 24ff.

Plumb adds a fear that unless historians will attend to this task of propaganda they will cease to be read and cease to play any part in their societies. Both manifestly confuse the problem of why men should be made to learn about history with the problem of the meaning of the past; or rather, to them only the particular meaning they extract from the past justifies the pursuit of history as an activity of the scholar and teacher.[29]

Let it be said at once that the underlying convictions behind the demands are in part sound. Historians cannot exist in a vacuum; they live in the society of men, influence it whether they like it or not, and should therefore be conscious of what they are about. But they should also be conscious of the dangers they run. It is all very well to regret the day when history was 'philosophy teaching by example', the day when historians thought themselves the moral preceptors of a ruling class and, aping Plutarch, used their science to instil high principles in their pupils. We cannot return to the attitude which produced a *Mirror for Magistrates* to show, by using historical instances, how those who offend against the divine order always come to a bad end;[30] and if we could return to it I doubt if many of us would. Yet such schoolmasterly ambitions are at the back of Dr Plumb's mind. When we take our more sophisticated history into the market place and the pulpit, we assume a task of some danger and must be almost pedantically careful of our integrity. Few, I daresay,

[29] Plumb, *Crisis in the Humanities*, 43: historians' 'explanations of the past should lead to an explanation of it for their time and generation, so that, by explaining, man's control over his future may be increased'.

[30] *The Mirror for Magistrates* (best edition by Lily B. Campbell, Oxford, 1938), a collection of cautionary tales mostly in verse, first published in 1559.

would wish to deride the conviction, expressed by that
not uneminent American historian, Conyers Read, who
some years ago told the American Historical Association
that 'the social responsibilities of the historian' involved
him in the defence of 'values'.[31] But how many would
agree with him that those values must be those of
American civilization and democracy, that the historian
plays a part in 'total war'? Since no man in society,
said Read, can escape some form of social control, the
historian must 'accept and endorse such controls as
are essential for the preservation of our way of life'.
Calling, in a fiery peroration, for the suppression of
inconvenient facts, he cried that if the historian will not
offer 'assurance that mankind's present position is on the
highway and not on some dead end, then mankind will
seek for assurance in a more positive alternative, whether
it be offered from Rome or from Moscow'.

Conyers Read was expressing too frankly what others
might wish to think, though it should be recorded that
he was fully and firmly answered by a fellow-historian
from a sounder American tradition.[32] Yet he was neither
fool nor knave, and he had thought as hard about his
professional purpose as Dr Plumb, with his more radical
predilections, has done. Read's case makes plain that
the historian's function in society cannot be reduced to
that of a preacher, whether he preaches the excellence
of all that is, or the necessity of reform, or the desir-
ability of revolution. If he is to be a good preacher he
must rest his case upon a faith; but if he is to be a
good historian he must question his own faith and
admit some virtue in the beliefs of others. If he allows

[31] *Amer. Hist. Rev.* lv (1949-50), 275ff.
[32] Howard K. Beale, 'The Professional Historian: His Theory
and His Practice', *Pacific Historical Review*, xxii (1953), 227ff.;
see esp. 254f.

the task of choosing among the facts of the past to deteriorate into suppression of what will not serve the cause, he loses all right to claim weight for his opinions. An historian may be an ex-businessman, as Read was, or like Gibbon an ex-captain of grenadiers, but when he pronounces upon economics or strategy we have a duty to judge him as an historian, and only as an historian. And there the simplicities of the preacher's call at once collapse.

The trouble with all these theories about 'the meaning of history' is twofold : the great range of contemporaneous events and the shortness of historical time permit of no convincing demonstration one way or the other. It is never difficult to see purpose or direction in a sequence of historical events if one confines oneself sufficiently, especially if one limits one's gaze to the winners in any conflict. Take the seventeenth century in England : few collections of years have had more 'purpose' inflicted upon them. If one looks at the struggles of the Stuart kings with their Parliaments, one readily writes the century's history as the story of growing liberty. If one concentrates on the problems of production and distribution, one sees the age as one of expanding trade, a growth in capitalist organization, increasing dependency (decline of liberty) for certain sectors of the population. If one looks at men's minds, one comes up with an explanation based on the secularization of thought and the development of the scientific approach. There is no obvious or provable connection between these lines of 'progress', and the historian who proceeds to make one— who, for instance, argues that political liberty was a precondition of intellectual advance and economic enterprise—can no more prove his case than the historian who refuses to see any such links. Moreover, he would be ignoring other things, such as the influence of the

Reformation or the central position of land-ownership. And then there is seventeenth-century France where political liberty on the whole declined, scientific thought flourished in different conditions and in its own, quite different, fashion, and economic life followed a different line towards increasing wealth as well as increasing strain. There is the rest of seventeenth-century Europe, not to mention Moghul India, Ch'ing China, or the kingdoms of tropical Africa. How can one possibly bring these varieties of experience into a scheme depending on a single line of progress? One can do it only by seizing on some development in subsequent history and elevating that to the sole significant position. This is not the legitimate activity of selecting the meaningful; it is the idle activity of forgetting the inconvenient. As for the shortness of historical time, I have already pointed out that recorded history amounts to no more than about two hundred generations. Even if there is a larger purpose in history, it must be said that we cannot really expect so far to be able to extract it from the little bit of history we have.

Still, Mr Carr and Dr Plumb claim to be able to discern it. They deny that they have fallen victim to the cruder fallacies of progress doctrines, those that identify what is with what must be, see in the past only the triumph of the present, and thus guarantee that high degree of self-satisfaction which was characteristic of whig historiography in England. Historians who adhere to a belief in progress are always liable to lapse from description into approval, to condemn the losers as blind or wicked, and to set the judicious garland of historical necessity on the victor's head. Mr Carr and Dr Plumb try to remember the variety of the past and claim that they give it due weight in the story. They

both assert that they are not determinists in the simple
sense of believing that the processes of history could
not have worked out differently from the way they did.
In this respect, however, it is difficult to treat them as
companions. Dr Plumb seems less concerned with the
question whether progress is really the lesson to be learned
from history than with his demand that it should be the
lesson taught by historians to their own age, in order
that the age may feel usefully optimistic. He trembles
on the precipice which swallowed up Conyers Read.
Mr Carr wishes to assert that an event like the Russian
Revolution not only happened in some measure necessarily (to him, the logic of history brought it about)
but in its happening testifies to the necessary improvement of mankind. That is to say, both concede a
measure of determinism in their thinking, but Dr Plumb
is not aware that it is there. Both are good enough
historians to avoid the more obvious traps of biased
selectivity and conditioned prejudice. In Mr Carr's
attitude to the Russian Revolution, and in Dr Plumb's
account of social amelioration, there is not only doctrine
but also much sound historical learning. Where they err
is not in their history but in their propaganda, in their
insistence that only their kind of interpretation will do.

Progress in history is in great part a matter of value
judgment, a personal matter, and though every competent historian can discover a measure of necessity in
events, none can prove that they are truly determined.[33]
If our authors see progress and necessity in history, they
are justified in saying so and in trying to persuade others
to agree with them. They are not justified in supposing
that no one can honestly see things in any other way
than in the light of their simplifying handtorch, and I

[33] Cf. Isaiah Berlin, *Historical Inevitability* (London, 1954).

object to their claim that history *must* be understood and proclaimed in their single fashion. For myself, I believe that they are wrong to concentrate so exclusively on the progressive and deterministic elements in the story. All talk about progress, if it does not simply mean change, rests on the assumption that the historian can tell what is better and what worse; but one man's better is usually another man's worse. I agree with Mr Carr and Dr Plumb that twentieth-century technology has greatly improved material life. I agree that in England, at least, social attitudes have in many ways grown better, that the nation is less given to violence and cruelty than once it was. I should, however, hesitate before supposing this to be a universal experience; and though, like Dr Plumb, I am temperamentally hostile to the school of thought which sentimentalizes the past and worships a chocolate-box substitute for the reality, I cannot forget that material progress has often been linked with deterioration, even material deterioration, in the quality of life,[84] and that the decline in active cruelty has been accompanied by a decline in active indignation against despotism and arbitrary rule. I do not pretend here to make an assessment or strike a balance, a thing each man must do for himself though the historian can assist him by illuminating the past; I only wish to point out that progress and necessity are doctrines which cannot be derived from, can only be superimposed upon, the study of history. And above all, I do not see why there should be only historians like Mr Carr and Dr Plumb, *laudatores temporis futuri*, why they should claim authority for their manifestly highly selective history, and

[84] Mr Carr (*What is History?*, 143ff.) comes very close to identifying technical progress with the expansion of true reason. One does not have to be a sentimentalist to regard this as a crude and misleading point of view.

why other points of view should be not so much con-
troverted as despised and condemned.

Does this then mean that there is no very positive
purpose in studying history, that it really is only a
matter of the student's private satisfaction? Are there
no standards by which one may call historians good
or bad, adequate or inadequate, right or wrong? I think
there are, but they cannot be discovered if the purpose
of history is approached from outside the discipline
itself. The sort of arguments put forward by Mr Carr
and Dr Plumb do not arise from their concern with
history but from their personal involvement in the
present and future of their own society.[85] This is comprehensible and can be creditable, but it in no way helps
to explain the purpose of studying history, and it begs
the question of what history means. Mr Carr and Dr
Plumb are, at heart, 'whigs', looking into the past for
reassurance; they begin with the assumption of a social
purpose stated (that the historian must offer to society
a demonstration of its power to advance itself) and they
then eliminate any use of history which does not
contribute to this purpose. For this reason they do fall
into the deterministic error of choosing from the variety
of history the line of events and detail which leads to
their own present position, their preconceived end; everything else, if they do not ignore it, they explain away.
The right approach would surely start from the other end.
We must first explain in what manner the past can
truly be studied—that is, we must accept the despised
tenet that the past must be studied for its own sake—
and then enquire whether this study has any contribution
to make to the present.

---

[85] I do not, of course, mean to deny that at other times they
are also very much concerned with history.

In short, we are once again faced with the autonomy of history : the study of history is legitimate in itself, and any use of it for another purpose is secondary. That secondary use will be laudable or deplorable in proportion as the autonomous purpose has been served well or ill. If I have rather more respect for the progress doctrines of Dr Plumb or Mr Carr than I have for the historical racialism of Rosenberg or the historical inevitabilities of Marxism, it is because I think their history better; if I have my reservations about their preferred interpretations, and especially about their prescriptions to other historians, it is because in my view they still ignore far too much about the past. The task of history is to understand the past, and if the past is to be understood it must be given full respect in its own right. And unless it is properly understood, any use of it in the present must be suspect and can be dangerous. One cannot use a corrupt means to a worthy end. And the creation of the sound instrument involves not only obvious things like doing the serious work of study, avoiding anachronism both in interpretation and judgment, devoting attention to the defeated as well as to the victors; it involves, above all, the deliberate abandonment of the present. The historian studying the past is concerned with the later event only in so far as it throws light on the part of the past that he is studying. It is the cardinal error to reverse this process and study the past for the light it throws on the present.

However, it does not in the least follow from this that the study of history, treated as autonomous and justified within itself, has no contribution to make beyond its frontiers. In the first place, let it be remembered that this pursuit of history in its own right is not only morally just but also agreeable. A good many people simply want to know about the past, for emotional or intellectual satisfaction, and the professional historian fulfils a useful 'social' function when he helps them to know better. He is also, of course, satisfying his own desire for knowledge, and he also is, after all, a part of society. This might be supposed to reduce the historian to a mere entertainer, but in fact it gives him a cultural role : he contributes to the complex of non-practical activities which make up the culture of a society. When he stimulates and satisfies the imagination he does not differ essentially from the poet or artist, which is not to say that he should be picturesque. There is an emotional satisfaction of a high order to be gained from extending the comprehending intelligence to include the past.

Next, it would certainly be untrue to suppose that history can teach no practical lessons. It enlarges the area of individual experience by teaching about human behaviour, about man in relationship to other men, about the interaction of circumstances and conditions in their effect upon individual and social fortunes. Its lessons are not straightforward didactic precepts, either instructions for action (the search for parallels to a given situation) or universal norms (history teaches that every thing progresses, history teaches the triumph—or futility —of moral principles); there is far too much variety about the past, far too much confused singularity about the event, to produce such simple results. Nevertheless, a sound acquaintance with the prehistory of a situation or problem does illumine them and does assist in making present decisions; and though history cannot prophesy, it can often make reasonable predictions. Historical knowledge gives solidity to the understanding of the present and may suggest guiding lines for the future.

Yet these emotional and practical uses of history are not its main contribution to the purpose of man. The study of history is an intellectual pursuit, an activity of the reasoning mind, and, as one should expect, its main service lies in its essence. Like all sciences, history, to be worthy of itself and beyond itself, must concentrate on one thing : the search for truth. Its real value as a social activity lies in the training it provides, the standards it sets, in this singularly human concern. Reason distinguishes man from the rest of creation, and the study of history justifies itself in so far as it assists reason to work and improve itself. Like all rational activities, the study of history, regarded as an autonomous enterprise, contributes to the improvement of man, and it does so by seeking the truth within the confines of its particular province, which happens to be the rational reconstruction of the past. In this larger purpose it has no sort of monopoly, for this it shares with every form of intellectual investigation, but it happens to have certain advantages in that it attracts a wide variety of intelligences, can do its work without too much demand on technical specialization in the learner, and can rest its capacity to train on its capacity to entertain.

In these advantages, which it possesses over both the natural and the social sciences, lie its temptations and perils : absence of technical specialization can lead to lack of rigour, entertainment to meretricious superficiality, variety of appeal to bias and propaganda. But the dangers do not deny the advantages; the possibility of corruption does not cast out the possibility of excellence. Integrity, resting on professional training and professional attitudes, is the safeguard. All historical work which satisfies the conditions of professional competence and integrity fulfils the historian's very important social duty; none that falls short of that standard can be trusted to fulfil any social duty safely, however conscious it may be of its obligations or however earnestly it may preach progress, the goodness of man, or the inevitability of revolutions. The quality of an historian's work must, as I have said, be judged purely by intellectual standards; the same is true of his contribution to society, though moral consequences may well flow from adherence to these principles of the reasoning capacity. It is not the problems they study or the lessons they teach that distinguish the historical sheep from the goats, but only the manner of their study, the precision of their minds, and the degree to which they approximate to the ultimate standards of intellectual honesty and intellectual penetration. *Omnia veritas.*

II

Research

The study of history, then, amounts to a search for the truth. But whether in fact such a thing as historical truth can exist has been a much debated problem; in particular, some philosophers, who show no sign of ever having tried to write history, like to arrive at the conclusion that, since historical knowledge cannot, strictly speaking, exist, there is no way of establishing truth in history.[1] These denials follow, as a rule, one of two lines of argument. They either maintain that the past, being dead and irrecoverable, cannot be known about in any meaningful sense; or that the impact of the historian upon his material renders all the history supposedly known a matter of private choice and interpretation, so that in the end there is nothing but subjective opinion, the very opposite to truth. Both these superficially cogent arguments betray an essential lack of acquaintance with the principles and practice of historical research, and it matters nothing that such relativist, even nihilist, views can sometimes be held by men generally regarded as historians. These opinions also show some ignorance of the matter studied by the historical discipline and forget that inability to know all

[1] For a sensible analysis, by a philosopher, of philosophical objections to the possibility of historical knowledge, see Arthur C. Danto, *Analytical Philosophy of History* (Cambridge, 1965), chs. 3-6.

the truth is not the same thing as total inability to know the truth.

1 The Possibility of Historical Truth

The problem of whether the past can be known at all—since it is not now here in the presence of the observer and cannot be brought back for study—arises from the attempt to make history seem a science, comparable in purpose and method to the natural sciences. The natural sciences have, it would seem, virtually abandoned the concepts of truth and falsehood; phenomena once regarded as objectively true are now seen to be only a statistical abstraction from random variables, and the accusing finger of the uncertainty principle further insists that, since observation alters a phenomenon, nothing is capable of being studied except after it is changed from the state in which it was meant to have been investigated. Practising scientists have therefore permitted the philosopher to remove the word true from their vocabulary and to substitute some such phrase as more probable, more accurately descriptive, more aesthetically or intellectually satisfying. This has not stopped scientists from continuing their efforts to investigate and understand nature, and in so far as it has reduced their positivist pride in the possession of the only strictly based truth the new philosophy may be thought of as gain. But historians have always been inclined to doubt the value, even the possibility, of their studies; they require not the new humility preached in the wake of Heisenberg, but some return to the assurance of the nineteenth century that the work they are doing deals with reality.

As a matter of fact, in a very real sense the study of

history is concerned with a subject matter more objective and more independent than that of the natural sciences. The common argument that, unlike the scientist, the historian cannot verify his reconstruction by repeating the experiment at will can be turned round to give him greater assurance of objectivity. Let it be granted that verifiability is the basis of the method employed by the natural sciences, and that in any acceptable sense it is clearly impossible for the historian. He can reconstruct in the mind, but he cannot re-enact. However, the fundamental reason for this disability ensures that his subject matter is to a remarkable extent quite independent of him. All scientific experiments are essentially constructs, and this applies to both the physical and the biological sciences. The scientist poses his problem, designs his experiment, and—if successful—can repeat problem, experiment and solution as often as he likes, just because he has himself determined the form in which the experiment is cast. Of course, he obtains his problem by asking questions of nature—of something outside himself—but his method enables him to treat nature wilfully and to compose for himself the argument which he wishes to resolve. Scientific experiments— dissection in taxonomic studies, for example, or the treatment of cells for purposes of study in biochemistry, or even the dropping of a stone from the tower of Pisa— are artificial; these things would not have happened but for a deliberate act of will on the part of the experimenter; the matter studied may be taken from nature, but before it is studied it is transformed for the purposes of the investigation. It is not going too far to assert that nearly all scientific study deals with specially prepared artificial derivatives from what naturally occurs.

The historian's case is very different. True, he may select his problems to suit himself. He may ask the questions he likes or believes capable of being answered; he may, and probably will, include himself in the equation when he explains, interprets, even perhaps distorts. But he cannot invent his experiment : the subject of his investigation is outside his control. When the problem of truth is under consideration, his essential difference from the natural scientist works in his favour. He cannot escape the first condition of his enterprise, which is that the matter he investigates has a dead reality independent of the enquiry. At some time, these things actually once happened, and it is now impossible to arrange them for the purposes of experiment. It may well be true that, for one reason or another, exactly what happened, or when and how and why, cannot now be known; no historian would suppose that his knowledge can be either total or finite. But this does not alter the fact that it is knowledge of a reality, of what did occur, not of something that the student or observer has put together for study. Just because historical matter is in the past, is gone, irrecoverable and unrepeatable, its objective reality is guaranteed : it is beyond being altered for any purpose whatsoever. Let it be noted that what is in question here is the subject matter of history, the events of the past, not the evidence they have left behind or the product of the historian's labours. However biased, prejudiced, incomplete and inadequate that product may be, it embodies an account of events that happened quite independent of the existence of him who now looks at them. Anyone who approves the tedious opinion that history is bunk does so because he prefers to ignore the reality of the past : but it is commandingly there, and the historian is not a free or purely wilful agent.

It follows from this that the historian's study is capable of concerning itself with a truth which is more absolute than mere truthfulness. Verifiability is the enemy of objective truth because it consists of the operation of the observer and experimenter upon the subject matter studied. The historian cannot verify; he can only discover and attempt to explain. In the work of discovery he has the assurance that he is looking for something that once had existence and is therefore, in theory, discoverable. We may not know precisely why William the Conqueror decided to invade England; we do know that he did invade and had a reason for doing so. We may argue over his invasion and its motive; we cannot argue them away. Nine hundred years ago they had existence; and just because they are irrecoverable in the flesh now, they are indestructible in the past reality. Thus while history will rarely be able to say : this is the truth and no other answer is possible; it will always be able to say : this once existed or took place, and there is therefore a truth to be discovered if only we can find it.

Whether the truth of these past realities is in fact discoverable is a question that shall be discussed later. So far, I have been concerned only to deny the charge that because the past cannot be re-enacted therefore there is, by definition, no such thing as historical truth. This leaves the second argument against the possibility of its existence, the argument that the past has neither meaning nor purpose, being merely a random accumulation of things and events, until subjectively ordered, by selection and arrangement, in the historian's mind.

What is here in question is not the truth, once again, of the historian's reconstruction, but his alleged inability ever to know a truth about the past because all he knows has had to pass through a cognitive process in his mind which inevitably involves selection, interpretation and perversion. An older, rather naïve, trust in the absoluteness of 'historical facts' has now been replaced by a general supposition that the facts of history are only historian's constructs, elevated among many other possible constructs to a special place of honour and importance. Mr Carr, in particular, who usefully reviews opinions on this issue, has made a very pretty distinction between facts as such and facts of history.[2] Though they are relevant, it would be only cruel to consider the really weak parts of his argument, especially his ignorance of the many things that can be discovered in ancient or medieval history. It is also unnecessary to do more than draw attention to the fundamental error he commits when he confuses the actuality of an event with the accident of the evidence surviving for it. But there is one passage in his discussion which summarizes his view of what makes a fact of history, and since this view, or something like its relativism, commands quite wide implicit approval it is worth a little analysis.

Mr Carr holds that there is a 'process by which a mere fact about the past is transformed into a fact of history'.[3] He quotes the case of a man who was killed by a rioting mob in 1850 and says that this event, once no fact of history at all, is on the way to becoming one because it has been mentioned in one book. It will achieve full status when it gets into one or two more historical accounts. The difference between facts about the past and facts of history hangs upon 'the element of interpretation' which the historian adds to the former in order to create the latter, though general acceptance of the interpretation offered is required before the fact's new status is secure.

This is really an extraordinary way of looking at history; worse, it is an extraordinarily arrogant attitude both to the past and to the place of the historian in

[2] *What is History?*, 10ff. [3] *Ibid.* 12.

studying it. A man was kicked to death in 1850: that is a fact, an event, which took place and which nothing now can either make or unmake. It is quite immaterial whether the fact is known to an historian or used by him in analysing a problem. If the event were unknowable—if no evidence of it had survived at all—it would certainly be neither fact about the past nor historical fact—it would have ceased to exist and that piece of potential history would never have materialized—but it would still, of course, have occurred, independent of any historian. However, the event can be known, and that is all that is required to make it a 'fact of history'. Interpretation, or general acceptance of a thesis, has nothing whatsoever to do with its independent existence. The point matters so much because Mr Carr, and others who like him think that history is what historians write, not what happened, come dangerously close to suggesting either that it does not much matter what one says because (interpretation being everything) there are always several reasonably convincing interpretations of any given set of events, or that history is altogether unknowable, being merely what happens to be said by a given historian at a given moment.

Mr Carr links his invention of special 'facts of history' with the by now conventional attack on Acton's programme for the old *Cambridge Modern History*. Certainly Acton was too sanguine when he supposed that 'ultimate history'—universally accepted and finally proven accounts of anything—would soon be possible. Though over a large range of historical problems this ambition will indeed never be achieved, the notion behind it was nevertheless true, for ultimate history is what actually happened, even though we shall never be able to rediscover it in full or with total assurance. Acton inferred from his positivist view of history that bias can be eliminated by strict attention to the facts and their meaning, so that in his cooperative history he hoped it would be hard to tell where a bishop left off and an agnostic took over. This demand has also received much ridicule, and Mr Carr duly laughs at it. Yet any reading of the old *C.M.H.* quickly shows that the ambition was fulfilled only too frequently, with a great increase in dullness and loss of life, but also a great increase in precision compared with what had been written before. That historians are prejudiced, blind and wilful, like any men, is true enough, and one may also agree that history written by men not afraid to allow themselves to appear in their discourse is both livelier history and probably better history. But that men cannot ever eliminate themselves from the search for truth is nonsense, and pernicious nonsense at that, because it once again favours the purely relativist concept of history, the opinion that it is all simply in the historian's mind and becomes whatever he likes to make of it.

Mr Carr's own work, and his reaction to criticism of it, prove conclusively that he does not in fact hold so whimsical a view of his profession. Yet his curious distinction between facts of the past and facts of history betrays two common failings: a lack of humility in the face of the past, and a confusion between the event and the meaning it acquires in the reconstruction attempted by the historian. The historian need not be too humble towards his fellows (though in an age of mass-reviewing and of jockeying for academic positions that is the humility he is likely to practise), but if he asserts a sovereignty over his facts he is a traitor to his calling. To say it once again: those things we discover, analyse, talk about, did actually once happen. They happened to real people, people quite as alive as we are and quite as entitled to respect for their humanity. They may not have known exactly what was happening, and historical interpretation and judgment are (as we shall see later) thoroughly legitimate activities : the historian is entitled to think about his discoveries and to find a significance in them which may well have been invisible at the time. But his doing so does not affect the independent reality of the event; the historian is not entitled to suppose that he alone, by choosing this fact and ignoring that, creates history. On the contrary, no investigator is more firmly bound by his material, less able to invent or construct the object of his study. This problem of the relationship between the genuine truth of the historical event and the discovery of that truth from the evidence left behind is the subject of this chapter.

2 *Facts and Method*

In denying the extreme relativism of which Mr Carr is only a recent and by no means an extreme exponent, I may well be taken to believe that facts about the past are simple, discrete, knowable entities which need only be collected in order that a structure called history may emerge. However, this naïve theory concerning the facts of history, possibly once widely current, has suffered sufficient bludgeoning to require no discussion here. But while no one will nowadays hold it in its naked simplicity, the time has come to point out that it has a little more validity than is usually supposed. In so far as it was ever believed, it was after all a theory of their enterprise developed by historians themselves, and some of those historians at least knew what they were doing. Its downfall has been largely the work of philosophers of history, psychologists and social scientists who certainly penetrated the weaknesses of the unreflective historian and showed him how unsatisfactory his often unconscious presuppositions were, but who did not as a rule try to write history. When, like R. G. Collingwood, they did, it is not possible to analyse their history in the terms of their philosophy : it is just ordinary sound history.

The effect of these anti-positivist criticisms has been to make it at present virtually axiomatic that historians never work with the materials of the past raw : some cooking process is supposed to have invariably intervened before the historian becomes even conscious of his facts. If that were so—if there were no way of knowing the knowable in its true state—historical truth would indeed become an elusive, possibly a non-existent, thing; one could at best then hope to find an historian learned, wise and sensitive enough to have cooked his materials in such a way that their natural flavour appears in the dish. That would still make the knowledge of history a matter of pure faith which, if it is to deserve the name of an intellectual discipline and to fulfil its social function of promoting the search for intellectual truth, it ought not to be. The theory differs from that already discussed in being more total and less arrogant. Where Mr Carr's relativism makes the historian the creator of history, this more subtle version of a similar relativism supposes more inexorably that the necessary intellectual processes involved in the study of history themselves interpose a barrier between the historian and the true reality of the past. But though more subtle, this second view is no more correct. The doubts comprised in it resolve themselves into two—the necessary existence of an observer and the necessary selection of evidence.

Is the historian ruled by some version of Heisenberg's uncertainty principle? Is it true that he cannot make contact with the historical fact without, by that very action, distorting it? The answer to this must be that, though in theory there is no need for this to happen, it is in practice a difficulty one should be aware of. The independent and real existence of historical events implies that, in theory at least, they can be observed absolutely, and for a very large number of somewhat basic facts this holds good. No matter how many observers may concern themselves with such questions as the day on which Britain declared war on Germany in 1914, who the eldest surviving child of Henry VIII was, or where Napoleon confronted the allied armies on a given day in 1813, they will all come up with the same answer. There is, in short, a very large body of agreed historical knowledge on which no dispute is possible, and though this body of knowledge may not by itself provide a very sophisticated interpretation of the past it is entirely indispensable to any study of it. One sometimes encounters among those who think about history a predilection for arranging facts in hierarchies. Mere dates or names—lists of kings and popes—are supposed to be more lowly than tables of trade statistics or the arguments used to defend a political philosophy. This is a game not worth the playing, for the peasants of this hierarchical society are as vital to it as its princes. Without the simple details of accurate chronology, genealogy and historical geography, history would have no existence. And of these simple facts an enormous number are precisely known.

However, while all the facts of history are theoretically in this knowable category, not all are so known, and as soon as more complex or private facts and events are involved the problem of the observer does arise. Different historians will differently regard the precise course of the battle of Hastings or the precise meaning of Hobbes's view of human psychology, not because they differently interpret agreed facts but because they see differences in the facts. The reason is plain enough: historical facts are knowable only by the evidence they leave behind, and in many cases that evidence is not clear-cut. To repeat, this is not a question of interpreting fact but of establishing it, and the differences resulting are likely to be differences in the degree and depth of knowledge, no more. Thus, for instance, anyone trying to establish, as Sir James Ramsay did, the totals of royal income and expenditure in the era of the Lancastrian kings, will resort to the receipt and issue rolls of the Exchequer. If, as Ramsay did, he takes them at their face value, he will total them up and suppose that he has the right answer. It takes a deeper knowledge of the material to understand that these totals are meaningless because the records contain quantities of repeated or fictitious entries. Thus the observer's understanding of his evidence will alter his historical knowledge, and increasing knowledge may also lead to a revision of supposedly established facts because facts do not occur in isolation. Most frequently, perhaps, the need for such revisions arises in connection with an ascription of originality. Wolsey, according to A. F. Pollard, created new machinery for the administration of the crown lands. However, since Pollard's day it has become clear that the machinery existed before Wolsey came to power and that he was responsible only for giving to existing arrangements the authority of an act of Parliament. This one change in the structure reverberates through any study of Wolsey's work which may end up by seeming quite differently inspired than it did when, in this one matter as well as in others, he appeared to be an administrative inventor. The historian's main 'uncertainty' lies in his ignorance; increasing knowledge genuinely produces increasing agreed certainty. This in itself proves that possibility of exact knowledge for which I am arguing and shows that differences of opinion may spring from differences in which the observer's personal intervention plays no part. Correct knowledge is not inherently impossible : it exists and constantly augments. In so far as variety of opinion reflects the move from ignorance to knowledge—and a great deal of historical debate amounts to just that—it firmly underlines the existence of real truth, not the prevalence of individual and arbitrary attitudes.

A more serious problem arises as soon as the historian proceeds from the establishment of a fact to the asking of complex questions. This is the notorious problem of the selection of evidence. The process of historical enquiry and reconstruction must work by means of selection. The mass of extant history cannot be rendered or even recorded without a deliberate choice by the historian, preserving this and discarding that. This is true of even the simplest forms of history. A medieval city chronicler will record outstanding events, such as deaths or floods or celebrations. Hundreds of men will have died that year within his knowledge, but he will commemorate a mere dozen. In so doing he applies a principle of selection : he answers the historically valid, if not very high-powered, question—who of importance died this year? Yet no two people may agree on the answer to this question. I may well wish to include my uncle and see no point in your second cousin, even if he did hold office as town scavenger. The very discovery of evidence depends on a selection of facts upon some principle of choice implicit in the question one asks, and there are therefore two variables involved at once : the question asked, and the arbitrarily determined choice. It is for this reason that some would deny the possibility of objective history at all and would claim that there is no history, only historians. In actual practice, however, the problem is not quite so devastating as it may appear in theory. We are often told that by the very act of asking a question the historian artificially limits his choice of material—that he finds in the evidence that for which he looks. Out of this limited range come further questions, themselves predetermined by the first question asked. The evidence is allegedly never in a position to play freely upon the enquiring mind, to suggest questions which are forced upon the historian, not forced by him upon the material. This sounds a convincing indictment, and there possibly are historians who proceed in this unsatisfactory way.[4] One can speak only from personal experience, and I must say that things do not happen quite like this.

The proper—and, as I believe, the common—way is different. The historian must certainly make one initial choice, of main area of study or line of approach. But after that (if he is worth considering at all) he becomes the servant of his evidence of which he will, or should, ask no specific questions until he has absorbed what it says. At least, his questions remain general, varied, flexible : he opens his mind to the evidence both passively (listening) and actively (asking). The mind will indeed soon react with questions, but these are the questions suggested by the evidence, and though different men may find different questions arising from the same evidence the differences are only to a very limited extent dictated by themselves. The part they themselves will play

---

[4] If the term historian were allowed to include the great system-makers, such as A. J. Toynbee, the indictment would obviously apply. But selection of evidence on that scale, to prove a fore-ordained case, removes the practitioner from the ranks of historians. Of course, his proper title may be more honorific : some people like prophets, especially of doom.

in these differences lies in different responses to the suggestions put out by the evidence. After this initial stage, the questions arising will be pursued specifically, and at this point the master-servant relationship is reversed. Now the historian specifically seeks evidence to answer his questions, and if his selection is ill-considered or too narrow he may introduce distortion. The interaction of the material and the questions asked of it is very intricate and sophisticated, but it is not true that in the proper pursuit of his study the historian's need to select destroys the independent existence of history. If that happens we are confronted by a bad historian writing bad history; but once again, the difficulty is not really inherent and can be overcome. There is no need to suppose that the bad or ill-trained historian is more typical than the good. This is not in the least to deny that the study of history depends on the asking of questions, or that the mass of historical facts acquires meaning only through being treated by the historian. It is to assert that the obvious dangers involved in this process can be provided for.

The two uncertainties of the historian—lack of knowledge, and the need to select—have their cure in the proper practice of scholarship and research. The methods of the trained professional historian are designed to protect him against his human difficulties, and they very often do achieve their purpose. Naturally, they do not render him immune to error, nor do they automatically eliminate bias and inadequacy, or the simple problems of time and space which hinder full or fully accurate knowledge. History is an unending search for truth, with the only certainty at each man's end that there will be more to be said and that, before long, others will say it. The historian's method does not give him the powers of a god, but it reduces the effects of human frailty and creates a formidable foundation of certainty beneath the errors and disputes which will never cease. Anyone doubting this might care to take any sizeable historical problem—the decline of the Roman Empire, or the rise of industrial England—and study its discussion in the serious literature of the last fifty years. He will encounter a great deal of disagreement, much proven error, and probably a fair amount of plain nonsense; but if he is at all alert he will be astonished by the way in which the body of agreed knowledge has augmented and by the manner in which variations of interpretation come to be first increased and then reduced by this advance. Historians are so fond of parading their disagreements—and the study does, indeed, progress as often as not by the reopening of seemingly settled questions—that the cumulative building up of assured knowledge of both fact and interpretation is easily overlooked. Yet it is indeed impressive, the product of systematic, controlled, imaginatively conducted research.

Two fairly common attitudes to historical research and method have done something to give the dog a bad name. On the one hand, there are the 'methodologists' who make a laborious and tedious science out of the historian's techniques, teaching it (as in some American graduate courses) almost as an independent discipline. On the other, we have the remaining inspired amateurs (this is an English failing) to whom the study of evidence presents no problems that cannot be solved by the common sense available to any reasonably intelligent man. Neither attitude has much to recommend it. The first turns a necessary tool into a nightmare mystery and is liable to produce egg-bound history or no history at all; the second promotes the exercise of prejudice and dilettantism, and is liable to produce pointless ephemera. There is further the difficulty that different fields of study, or different periods of history, seem to require methods of their own; but to think so represents the not uncommon confusion between method and technique. In fact, every historian needs to master some techniques, that is to say, he needs to know some technical tools which help him understand his material. Certainly the medievalist's palaeography, diplomatic, knowledge of Latin, understanding of lost administrative and legal processes are skills more obviously technical than those required of the historian of the nineteenth or twentieth centuries; they are, moreover, techniques requiring to be formally taught and capable of being so taught, which is not quite so true of the basic techniques used in investigating modern diplomatic history, though the problems, for instance, of modern economics require some highly technical learning. The best known training schools for historians, as the École des Chartes in Paris, the various national schools at Rome, or the London Institute of Historical Research, have consequently been dominated by medievalists who have reduced their techniques to a teachable science, and historians of more recent times have, understandably but mistakenly, reacted like Renaissance humanists confronted by the subtle and tedious irrelevancies of the schoolmen. Yet all these techniques—whether palaeography or statistics, medieval law or modern technology—are only particular aspects, conditioned by the surviving evidence, of the historical method which itself is the same for all historians.

Historical method is no more than a recognized and tested way of extracting from what the past has left the true facts and events of that past, and so far as possible their true meaning and interrelation, the whole governed by the first principle of historical understanding, namely that the past must be studied in its own right, for its own sake, and on its own terms. It is a way of turning the evidence to account, and though there is nothing mysterious about it, it is nevertheless rigorous and not to be confused with the so-called common-sense approach of the intelligent but untutored enthusiast. Its fundamental principles are only two, and they may be expressed as questions, thus : exactly what evidence is there, and exactly what does it mean? Knowledge of all the sources, and competent criticism of them—these are the basic requirements of a reliable historiography. This essay can attempt no specific description of historical technique; that is a large subject of its own, covered in some useful textbooks.[5] This demonstration that history can be 'scientifically' studied must not be burdened with systematic instructions to intending practitioners; it must concentrate on analysing the working principles of the method, in order to show that it does indeed overcome the difficulties interposed between the historian's search and the truth of history.

3 The Sources

To know all the evidence. Ideally the student should never consider less than the total of the historical material which may conceivably be relevant to his enquiry. Though in many circumstances this will be an impossible counsel of perfection, it remains the only proper ambition. One of the demands embodied in it can, in any case,

[5] E.g., on a descending scale of size : J. G. Droysen, *Grundriss der Historik* (first published, Leipzig, 1868, often reprinted); C. V. Langlois and C. Seignobos, *Introduction to the Study of History* (English translation, London, 1898); C. G. Crump, *History and Historical Research* (London, 1928); M. Bloch, *The Historian's Craft* (English translation, Manchester, 1954); G. Kitson Clark, *Guide for Research Students Working on Historical Subjects* (Cambridge, 1958).

always be observed: the historian must know the range and types of sources available to him, and he must have done his utmost to learn what has been written in and around the topic with which he is concerned. In other words, he must learn to compose a full bibliography of his subject and keep it up to date. Knowing what other historians have written is vital to a proper job, even though in the present context of explaining the connection between the historian and historical truth it has little importance. But knowing one's fellow-workers at first hand is not only a sensible precaution to prevent needless duplication or the repetition of exploded error; it also assists in covering the range of the sources, suggests questions, and opens lines of fruitful discussion. That it can in addition provide the relief of disputation, anger and abuse is a further but accidental gain to writer and reader alike.

However, what matters are the sources, that is to say the physical survivals from the events to be studied. And here the first demand of sound historical scholarship must be stressed: it must rest on a broad-fronted attack upon all the relevant material. Historical research does not consist, as beginners in particular often suppose, in the pursuit of some particular evidence which will answer a particular question; it consists of an exhaustive, and exhausting, review of everything that may conceivably be germane to a given investigation. Properly observed, this principle provides a manifest and efficient safeguard against the dangers of personal selection of evidence. Where there is a manageable amount of material, either because the question is very restricted (for instance the administration of a particular estate over a limited number of years) or because little enough has survived (as in most of the problems with which ancient history deals), the prescription can be followed to the letter. Not

that even here it is always easy. To take our examples:
studying one estate may involve studying a great many
others if the special case is to make sense, and the
ancient historian, spared an abundance of written evidence, may *inter alia* have to assimilate the work of
the archaeologists, possibly on the ground. Nor need we
forget the very different obstacles raised by the survival
of too little evidence. Still, anybody working in any
aspect of European history before, say, A.D. 1100 should
find it possible to see everything that bears on his
problem; and though materials rapidly increase in bulk
thereafter the task can still, as a rule, be discharged.
But it cannot be discharged once the historian enters
the nineteenth century. Indeed, from about 1450 on-
wards there are many large issues of historical investigation for which the rule that all the evidence be searched
becomes so full of difficulty that the daily sufferings of
the historian of recent times are, at least in some
measure, also familiar to his colleague working on the
earlier periods.

No doubt, the austere answer would be that when all
the evidence cannot be seen that piece of history cannot
be written. This might have the possible advantage
of freeing the world from a good deal of so-called contemporary history, but it is clearly not an acceptable
solution to say that the writing of history must wait for
neglect, accident, water, fire and rats to do their work of
rendering the labour possible by reducing the evidence
to piecemeal obscurity. Historians must be able to produce
sound and trustworthy history even in circumstances
which do not permit them to see everything; there
should be rules of scholarship applicable in such very
common cases to ensure that even a partial view of the
evidence avoids the uncertainties of personal selection.

It is one of the shortcomings of more recent history

that its practitioners, overwhelmed by the task of mere study, have done almost nothing so far to work out proper rules of this kind. The most obvious solution of the dilemma consists of relying on the preliminary work of others. This can mean taking other historians' writings on trust, an expedient so desperate as hardly to deserve the name; but it may occasionally be necessary if anything is to be done at all. In practice, of course, all historians gain information from the work of others : but some check on the methods of even the best established and reputed of scholars—some sample-testing of their use of evidence—is always advisable. More satisfactory are short-cuts to the material, where these exist. Thus for considerable stretches of English history the enquirer is provided with lists and calendars of documents which he could never in a life-time work through himself. Naturally, much depends on the manner in which the work is carried out, and the accumulated experience of scholars quite quickly establishes degrees of reliability or completeness in these predigested forms of the evidence. Again, however, some genuine rules apply : the criteria are by no means purely subjective.

Such ground-clearing operations are the better the more closely they adhere to the state of the material as they found it and the less they permit an editor to intrude. Thus the least dangerous of them are those that take a given body of records and without rearranging it present it in abstracts, as is done, for instance, in the *Calendar of Patent Rolls* or the *Calendar of State Papers Domestic*. Here the historian gets an accurate list of the material which can be used as an index to the originals, so that the overwhelming mass is reduced to manageability. Less satisfactory, and full of dangers to be remembered, are calendars which comprise materials chosen by the editor on some non-archival principle.

The famous *Calendar of Letters and Papers of Henry VIII*, for instance, collected in chronological order all the material for the reign which its compilers could find or accommodate. In other words, the calendar was intended not as a guide to the sources but as a replacement of them, a point underlined by the very full abstracts used; and indeed, a good deal of the history of the period has been written in reliance on these printed abstracts only. Since the work was done competently and, on the whole, with integrity (there are exceptions to both qualifications), the calendar proved not only usable and useful but also produced some valuable history, as in A. F. Pollard's massive work which rested entirely on its existence and dispensed with manuscripts altogether. But the manner of its composition was responsible for two traps characteristic of the method and quite independent of any bias in the compiler. Since it did not simply describe one existing archive, it gave a quite misleading impression of completeness; and since its makers rearranged their materials in a pattern chosen by themselves (in this case chronological) they destroyed the original arrangement and deprived the historian of much important knowledge. The provenance of documents—the way in which they came to be produced and deposited—is one of their most telling aspects, and this is something that, disastrously, cannot be established from that calendar.[6] These are serious deficiencies in the production of competent men; if in addition the compiler was inadequate—if he neither understood the way in which the material had been created, nor the importance of presenting it

[6] In this instance the originals do not assist because some devil prompted the Public Record Office to rebind their share of the material—the greater part of what was used—in the order of the calendar.

in a neutral manner, nor possibly even the real meaning of his records—he could, as W. A. Shaw did in his *Calendars of Treasury Books and Papers*, frustrate his enterprise and obscure the evidence he meant to render accessible. When materials become too many to be read in full, short-cuts not only may but must be used, but always with a full appreciation of their shortcomings and not forgetting that there is a difference between the whole and its parts. In practice this means two things. The historian should, so far as possible, use these productions as guides to the originals : he should with their help limit his area of search, not confine it to the printed aid. And he should treat them as he would treat all his evidence, by subjecting them to critical study : he must know how they came into being.

In any case, for large areas of history no such aids exist, and here the choice would seem to lie between the impossible (reading everything) and the undesirable (giving up work). At the perfectionist level the dilemma is inescapable, but at the perfectionist level action always ceases. We are seeking that possible which remembers and approaches the ideal. The problems of the historian faced with too much material are no more insoluble than those of the historian frustrated at every turn by the absence of evidence; neither can ever be made truly happy, but both can continue to strive.

The problem of abundance can, up to a point, be managed by controlled selection, that is to say by choosing on principles which have nothing to do with the real question asked or the ultimate product. To begin by selecting in answer to specific questions introduces the arbitrary, the personal and uncertain, and the first selection should therefore rest on different grounds determined by the material itself. It should arise from a total survey of the material and be systematic with reference to it, not to the historian's purpose. Thus an historian landed in this 'recent history' predicament should acquaint himself in general with the categories of evidence available in his field of study and then concentrate on the fundamental. If, for instance, he wishes to study the manner in which English government after about 1840 came to concern itself with public health, he will soon learn that important evidence is found in parliamentary papers, newspapers, memoirs, biographies, and the resources of municipal archives. But he is likely also to realize that the first basis of his research lies in the records of certain government departments, and he might therefore make a systematic study of these. Even so, severe limitations, for instance of the time covered, may become necessary. Once he has really worked through this class of documents, he can apply the method of selection by answer to specific questions to the rest of the ground with the degree of safety and objectivity produced by the exhaustive study of a body of 'master' records. Control of choice—reliability in the choice—depends on a high standard of professional learning which alone overcomes the perils of the amateur's pick-and-choose method; and it can be achieved only by a really thorough study of a body of material chosen not because it all contributes to the solving of a particular problem but because it has the organic unity arising from a particular archive-producing process.

None of this may sound very satisfactory, and there need be no doubt that the quality of the historian will always determine the quality of his research. Nevertheless, the procedure outlined reduces this personal element and offers valuable safeguards because it depends on two things: a real training in the craft practised, and a real concern with history (the past as such) rather than with the formulation of theories about it. No procedure can guarantee invariable soundness, but some are more likely to produce it than others. And when the obstacle to success lies in the imposed necessity of severe selection, the safeguard lies in the separation of selection from conclusion, in delimiting the area of enquiry in the first place by criteria different from those which determine the ultimate selection of the material used to solve the problem posed.[7] The rule has an inhibiting consequence which to some will seem to render it stultifying: it strongly urges that, for the present at least, work in insufficiently explored regions, overwhelmingly equipped with material, should confine itself to the study of very restricted topics. Certainly it would seem sensible to make clearings in the forest before laying out the garden. However, this goes counter to one dubious and one legitimate desire. The dubious predilection is for the study of large tracts in outline because this seems more important, more impressive, better worth while, more likely to lead to fame than any detailed investigation of limited bits of the past; in the laity, in particular, though not only there, one meets a strong enough inclination to call no one historian who does not sweep and survey. Unfortunately people will not believe that bird's-eye views are strictly for the birds. Some who should know better sometimes give support to such anti-scholarly views, as did Hugh Trevor-Roper

[7] It has always been plain to anyone engaged in training historians that the trade is learned better in manageable areas. This supports the view that it would be nice if historians of recent times could bear to be trained as medievalists, acquiring the competence to handle tools where the techniques are better developed and the paths more clearly blazed. Thereafter they could take their training to new pastures. But few men, thoroughly soaked in the waters of one historical pond, feel inclined to swim in another.

who in his inaugural lecture as Regius professor at Oxford, appeared to identify precise research with a narrow mind and a pettifogging dullness.[8] The more legitimate objection to avoiding the big book is that without attempts to see aspects of recent history as some sort of a whole, without some effort to fit together a story and a synthesis, the problems which need answers and whose solution could advance real understanding of the whole do not become apparent. This is perfectly true and justifies the writing of 'premature' general studies, provided it is remembered that their chief purpose should be to define the work of further investigation which waits to be done.

Nevertheless—and without overlooking the dangers of the narrow mind and the petty concern, about which more shall be said in the next chapter—in regions of superabundant material the real work of discovering historical truth must for quite a while concentrate upon particular studies of restricted problems. Ultimately, the man who has proved his trustworthiness and professional skill in this kind of labour not only has a right to be heard on what he cares to say on a larger topic or by way of creative synthesis: he will have deserved confidence. It is one of the principles of historical research, proved by experience but unprovable in any other way, that a genuine training and mastery obtained by systematic work on a restricted body of material will show themselves in producing instinctive rightness when bodies of material too enormous to be fully worked through are tackled in a more superficial or selective way. Those

[8] H. R. Trevor-Roper, *History Professional and Lay* (Oxford, 1957), esp. 12-13. Ph.D. theses—Mr Trevor-Roper's special target—may reflect a narrow and pettifogging mind; grand sweeps may demonstrate shallow and superficial glibness. Neither deficiency is ineluctably wedded to a particular method of working.

likely to be put off by the mountains rising before them can take comfort in the fact that one mountain is much like another; real acquaintance with a part of the range enables the explorer to tell much more about the rest without walking all over it than at first he would have supposed possible.

4 Evidence and Criticism

There is no perfect substitute for total acquaintance with the relevant material, even as there is no perfect way of overcoming severe losses of evidence. Thus there is no absolutely satisfactory way of studying history, which to some may put the subject out of court, but to others, unwilling to see an end to their metier, may seem its chief attraction. In any case, it is not enough to have seen everything; a mere accumulation of pebbles does not make a building, or even a highway. It is certainly even more important that everything seen should have been looked at in the proper light. If the independent reality of history is ever to be apprehended, the real meaning of the surviving material must be elicited from the surface appearance. Once the first stage of discovering the evidence has been got through, the methods of historical research boil down to the orderly and controlled assessment of it. Here again, common sense is not quite enough.

A good deal has been written on the criticism of sources, and some have tried to reduce it to scientific accuracy. There is good reason why historians should convince themselves and others that their way with sources enables them to establish, or at least come very near to establishing, the kind of truth which, I have argued, lies behind the history we find in books.

The laity—and this is liable to include professional
academics in other disciplines—take a good deal of
persuading that the historian can really tell what happened and why. Marc Bloch was driven to such exasper-
ation by uninformed scepticism that the largest part of
his unfinished *The Historian's Craft* turned into a
practical description of the use of evidence quite as
puzzling to the uninitiate as silence on the subject would
have been. Not so long ago, the B.B.C. televised a
play called 'Lloyd George knew my Father' which had
much fun at the expense of historians sadly misled by the
deliberate destruction, invention and perversion of
evidence provided, for historical use, by the actors in
some imaginary scandal. Neither author nor audience
appeared to know that this is a commonplace problem
to the historian for which he has time and again found
solutions. The whole training of the historian is designed
to help him dispose of deliberate manufactures. He may
not be, and the professional historian too often is not,
brought up to understand imaginatively and sympatheti-
cally, but he is certainly taught to be critical and
sceptical, sometimes too much so. True, mistakes are
frequent enough, and evidence can be misinterpreted. I
often wonder what the illustrious dead make of all the
things historians discover about them; if the Elysian fields
ring with Homeric laughter, a continued interest in historical writing may well be the cause. But this is, at
once, to display that excessive scepticism which lies at
the heart of every sound historian and must be guarded
against. That the truth can be extracted from the
evidence by the application of proper principles of
criticism should not be doubted, any more than that the
enterprise will not always succeed.

Criticizing the evidence means two things : establishing
its genuineness, and assessing its proper significance. The

first is largely a technical problem. Forgeries have been successful in their time, but sooner or later they have got found out, from the Donation of Constantine to the Protocols of the Elders of Zion.[9] As a matter of fact, big forgeries of this kind are rare; producing them is much too laborious a business and only to be undertaken for some very cherished purpose. Altogether the deliberate manufacture of historical evidence is extremely uncommon; few people seem to think it worth their while to invent a documented history for themselves, or perhaps they find distortions and pretence in their otherwise genuine memoirs adequate. Why have we no false testaments of Napoleon or forged policy statements of Ghengis Khan? A distinction must be made : a spurious document is one written by someone other than the pretended author or at some time other than that pretended in it. False statements produced at the alleged time and by the alleged author are lies and require a different treatment.

It may in general be said that no one ever forged evidence to deceive historians; the intention, nearly always, is to deceive contemporaries, and most commonly a court of law. Financial statements and title deeds are the main preoccupation of the forger, and medieval charters the best example. According to V. H. Galbraith, 'forgery was the medieval monk's peccadillo', and his motive as a rule was to supply evidence of rights which he, or his house, regarded as perfectly well established but which unfortunately were not founded upon genuine

[9] Although it was not until Lorenzo Valla's famous attack in the early fifteenth century that the spurious Donation was generally exposed for the fraud it was, the facts were apparently well known to papal officers by the late tenth century (W. Ullmann, *A History of Political Thought: the Middle Ages*, Harmondsworth, 1965, 98n.).

deeds. The impulse to rectify the unfortunate deficiencies of the muniment room in the interests of true possession was generous and understandable, and if it has given medievalists many a happy hour distinguishing false from genuine it has had long-term beneficial effects. Nowadays, the techniques involved in this sorting are sufficiently established (ability to do this work does not prove possession of the higher intelligence), but it should be remembered that even thirteenth-century judges could apply such scientific tests as the search for discrepancies between alleged dates and the design of the seal, or for errors in royal styles mistakenly antedated by the forger. The historian needs only to establish the correct form and context of the genuine document in order to be able to detect the false, and this is rarely a problem once he leaves off using printed editions (though good editors will do the job for him) and looks at originals.

A good example of what should not happen was provided by R. B. Merriman in his edition of Thomas Cromwell's letters. In that collection, nos. 163 and 180 appear to be blackmailing notes from Cromwell to priors of monasteries allegedly saved from suppression by the minister; they have consequently loomed large in the usual denunciations of him.[10] There is nothing in the edition to raise doubts. But one glance at the originals shows that they were written and signed in a hand quite different from that of Cromwell or any of his clerks; that is to say, they were bits of private enterprise on someone's part who hoped to cash in on the minister's position and reputation, and since they were found among Cromwell's papers we may suppose that the trick was discovered and the minister informed. Read

[10] R. B. Merriman, *The Life and Letters of Thomas Cromwell* (Oxford, 1902). Even Dom David Knowles was taken in (*Religious Orders in England*, iii. 337).

rightly, these letters therefore tell in his favour, not
against him. As forgeries they present no problem at all,
and that would generally seem true of such documents.
Admittedly, successful forgeries by definition escape
detection, but it is neither apparent nor likely that this
happens at all frequently. The evidence suggests that
successful deception is very difficult, that it is practised
for immediate and usually financial purposes and not
in order to influence historical accounts, and that the
techniques for establishing genuineness are sufficiently
refined to cope with it. This is not to say that the
historian should not be on the alert for forgery; there
is probably no record-using historian living who has
not at times wondered about the genuineness of some
document before him. The rules are simple : if it can
be proved genuine by internal and external evidence,
use it; if such evidence shows it clearly to be forged, use
it with that knowledge in mind (that is, it now means
something different); if there is doubt about it, discard it.
The true forger is not a serious enemy to the truth-
seeking historian.

Genuine evidence, however, poses every sort of problem, and it is now necessary to agree with the well-
established opinion that while the facts of history may
exist in their own right they come to use and notice
through the mind of the historian who selects, interprets
and employs them. What guarantee can there be that
one historian's opinion or interpretation is better than
another's? What are the principles of scholarship upon
which safe knowledge can stand?

There is a single question which the researcher must
ask himself in assessing his evidence : how and why did
this come into existence? From the historian's point of
view, all evidence divides into two kinds : that produced
specifically for his attention, and that produced for

some other purpose. What survives from the past was put together either by someone who wished it to survive, or by someone who had a purpose to serve in which the prospect of the historian's interest played no part. The first comprises in the main evidence of a literary and often secondary kind : chronicles, memoirs, notes of self-justification, letters intended for publication. To the second category belong pretty well all documents and records, most but not all letters and state papers, official memoranda whether published or not, reports of commissions and of lawsuits—the products of policy, business, and the ordinary events of life—but also the material relics of past societies, such as buildings or artefacts. These lists are not exhaustive; the categories are, and the historian should always first become clear with which of the two he is dealing. His task differs according as he faces an attempt to influence and persuade his like or an attempt to influence men long dead—or sometimes, to influence nobody. Material in the first category, being designed to affect the writing of history, can be judged with relative ease. The purpose which produced it was rational and therefore identifiable; the interests of the producer can usually be ascertained without trouble. Whether actor or himself historian, he is likely to have a case to make : his case once determined, one can judge both his own production and the material which he provides accordingly.

Things are rather more complicated with evidence of the second kind—far and away the most important and common. At first sight it might seem that a financial account, the record of a court case, or a house cannot bring trouble to the historian; as long as he can read or recognize them, they will, since they were never meant to deceive him, tell him the truth. But the point is, on the one hand, that to see them is not necessarily to understand them, and on the other that they may well have been intended to deceive someone else. A proper understanding of a given document involves separating the specific from common form and grasping the process by which it came into existence. It is here that professional learning comes into its own; only full ranging knowledge of what occurs in the papers of a given period or problem will prevent misapprehensions.

A few examples will show this best. In the Tudor Star Chamber, complainants invariably charged the opposing party with a violent or riotous act; but since this was requisite if the court was to have jurisdiction, it may be no more than a matter of form. On the other hand, it may record a real event; only the experienced student, weighing up the various documents in the case, will be able to arrive at a reasonably safe opinion whether the assault and disturbances had really taken place. Thomas Cromwell almost invariably signed himself as his correspondent's 'loving friend'; it would be extraordinarily rash to base any deductions as to relationship or personal feelings on that phrase, though something may quite possibly be inferred from its absence. That eminent historian, A. F. Pollard, encountering in fifteenth-century royal grants the phrase 'datum de mandatu parliamenti', concluded that Parliament had authorized the gift; but the words were common form and referred to the dating of the grant which, by a statute of 1444, was appointed to be the date of the delivery of the authorizing warrant into the king's Chancery. In the accounting system of the English Exchequer, 'arrears' represented unpaid items of revenue supposedly due to the king but often irrecoverable; they were carried over from year to year and swelled totals, if these were given at all; failure to recognize this would sadly pervert any calculation of the crown's revenue.

Every field of history yields examples of this kind, and only training—acquired knowledge—can save the historian from obvious howlers and bad misjudgments. On the other hand, such training saves him with ease. The understanding of all evidence depends on a proper apprenticeship in its use. The student would do well to suppose that he does not grasp the true meaning of his material until he has thoroughly acquainted himself with the organization that produced it, the purpose for which it was produced, and the difference between common form and the exceptional.

This phase of the job needs instruction and should receive it. The question of false intent needs intelligence and should receive that. Obviously a great deal of historical evidence now extant was at the time of its production intended to create a given effect. Diplomatic correspondence is a good case in point : communications to foreign governments can prove very revealing when placed side by side with instructions to one's own representative. Few would take expressly propagandist literature at its face value. But the matter can be less obvious, as in the letters of honourable men presenting some view of themselves to others, in the *ex parte* statements of litigants, or in legislation serving given interests but justified on grounds of general utility. Here the historian, trained to a critical scepticism, is on the whole unlikely to surrender to the bias of his sources; at least, the professional is not. Instead he faces, curiously enough, two difficulties working the other way. One is this very scepticism. It is all too easy to see deep deviousness in everything and to doubt the apparent meaning of every piece of evidence. However wise it may be to question motive at all times, and however capable of deliberate perversion all men may be, it remains a fact of experience that simplicity, straightforwardness and transparency also exist. The historian cannot therefore proceed on any single line of judgment; his mind must be forever open to the two possibilities that the evidence means what it says and that it does not mean what it says. To achieve as secure a judgment as possible, the historian here requires his most rare and almost most dangerous gift : an all-embracing sympathy which enables him, chameleon-like, to stand with each man in turn to look upon the situation. The gift is dangerous because it may in the end bring him to a total inability to judge or even to make up his mind; it need not do so but it often does.

In practice, too many historians here allow bias to intervene. They finish up by believing those they are inclined to and doubting the rest. Take, for example, the various conspiracies against the government of Elizabeth I. Among the traditional Protestant historians, it was taken for granted that Catholics, and Jesuits in particular, justified all means by reference to the end and thus were evidently always engaged in deep deviousness and double thinking. Of course they would plot. Therefore the word of the government's police was always to be accepted when it indicated that treasonable conspiracies had been uncovered. More recent Catholic historians have inverted the principle of judgment : it is now sometimes taken for granted that Elizabethan statesmen were 'Machiavellian', so that of course Sir Francis Walsingham's 'discoveries' were all in fact carefully engineered and the alleged conspiracies were organized, for its own purposes, by the Queen's government. In consequence both sides have displayed a remarkable respect for the other's supposed powers of deception and convoluted plotting, as well as more obviously a naïve trust in the honesty of their own champions. They make the enemy appear devilish clever, while their own side come close to being holy fools. A less committed attitude would treat them both as humans of the more familiar kind; it would quickly discover that neither side was invariably 'Machiavellian' or invariably incapable of deceit. Genuine plots, with all the purposes ascribed to them by the government, existed all right, but the Queen's agents fostered them further in order to discover and exploit all their ramifications. Both sides behaved as a reasoned reflection would expect them to behave : one, despairing of overthrowing a Protestant queen in any other way, sought to organize subversive violence, while the other, convinced that such dangers existed, magnified them and even encouraged the more inept plotters in order to squash them the more successfully. This case demonstrates well how all-round sympathy and understanding (a form of impartiality) can unravel the problems of the evidence; but though obvious it is also typical.

Excessive scepticism must therefore be guarded against as much as a childlike trust, especially as both reactions (two sides to the one coin of insufficient thought) are liable to be called forth by the historian's private, and sometimes unconscious, attitudes. A more serious and probably insurmountable difficulty lies in the fact that all assessment of evidence must be the work of the intellect, of the reasoning faculty. The historian cannot but work on the assumption that whatever happened is capable of a rational explanation and that evidence is the product of an act discoverable by reason. And yet we all know that this is not quite true, that we act, react and even reflect from motives which have little to do with reason and under influences—such as ill-health, a quarrel with people not involved in the transaction, whim and lack of thought—that can but rarely appear in the results of action, that is, in the evidence. Though at times these untouchables in history may become known to us, as a rule they do not; and we remain ignorant of them at the very times when, being most accidental, they would be most influential. Some historians, and above all biographers, therefore believe that a knowledge of psychology (especially of morbid psychology) is indispensable, with the result that one too often encounters some pretty awful bits of Freudian or post-Freudian commonplaces in the analysis. I do not discount the value of a real knowledge of the springs of human action, provided it is used with an almost excessive caution and with an overriding respect for what is actually there in the evidence. However, such methods are themselves fundamentally rational because they apply reason even if they deal with the non-rational; at best they reduce the area of uncertainty created by men's unwillingness always to act rationally, and at worst they greatly enlarge it. Yet on balance this matters little in most cases: over a series of actions or events, the irrational, so to speak, levels out, and a reasoned analysis can discover the truth. The difficulty does not, in fact, arise so much in the most obvious instances. It may be true that Napoleon's behaviour during the Waterloo campaign was influenced by deteriorating health and an increasing inability to judge reality, but in part these elements can be assessed and in part they vanish in the fact that the campaign was also based on perfectly rational, if erroneous, decisions.

The historian's predilection for the rational explanation causes most trouble when the evidence is thin or non-existent. Thus one would often like to know the forces or groups behind a piece of legislation, and it is natural to assume that interests benefited by a law were also instrumental in demanding it. Yet where the evidence exists, it often shows that men do not by any means always recognize their own interests: the facts of the past as well as experience in life occasionally demonstrate that the simple equation of interested party and instigator can break down. Rather than base his argument on the identification of reasonable conjecture with ascertained fact, the historian ought to be aware of the difficulty and admit ignorance. Not everything can be known, and the historian, since he deals with men, must concede the limits of rationality. However, reason also exists and men do act upon it, consciously, much of the time; again, as in the case of proper scepticism, the answer lies in maintaining a balance controlled by a rigorous study of the evidence, in considering the probable and possible as well as the obvious, and in avoiding oversimplification one way or another.

All this, no doubt, might help to confirm the belief that, no matter what has been said here, historical knowledge is strictly speaking not possible. It may be available in an ideal and theoretic fashion since that which is to be known is real; but it can never be available in practice because the interposition of the historian's personality and his inability to re-enact the event introduce too many variables. It must therefore be reasserted that these uncertainties by no means cover the ground: a great deal of history, simple and basic as well as more complex, is knowable and known beyond the doubt of anyone qualified to judge. In another very large sector, the proper techniques of the trained professional establish further secure knowledge, and constant work of research is all the time adding to that established knowledge. The rest of the field contains some things that may never be known and a great many more of which knowledge will never be so certain that disputes will cease. For the reasons already stated, this is particularly true of motive, of the reasons behind action, thought and speech. But even in this region we are not simply at the mercy of individual historians and their idiosyncrasies; here, too, rules apply, though these rules depend more extensively on the historian's abilities than do those which govern the detection of forgery or the understanding of individual pieces of evidence.

5 *Imagination*

The ultimate problem of historical evidence, as has often been recognized, is that none of it occurs in isolation. The interaction and interdependence of things are so manifest that some would doubt whether 'fact' is a term of meaning in history. Once again, this may be a perfectly justified tenet for the philosopher; the working historian, enquiring what the law was in a given dispute, how much a man was paid by way of salary, which of two particular despatches embodied the real policy of a government, which specific road was used by some army on a stated day (and all these are legitimate and important questions in the reconstruction of history) must answer the philosopher's doubt in the manner of Dr Johnson's reply to Berkeley. Yet at the same time, the working historian is even more aware than the philosopher that every question he asks involves him in a congeries of facts and specific details, that even if the final answer is a single figure or place or name, he has got there by means of a great many other figures and places and names as well as other parts of the evidence. However controlled his selection, it is still selection; however full his evidence, it is never complete; however impartial his assessment, it is still *his* assessment. Is there then no ultimate standard, independent of the historian, which applies as soon as the matter becomes more complicated?

The frank answer to this is that no absolute standard can, or perhaps should, exist, but once again it must be added that the trained and experienced mind comes so close to one that on the, as it were, Newtonian level of the universe historical truth is ascertainable. The discovery of truth requires not only the equipment already discussed—acquaintance with the available evidence and scholarly assessment of it—but also imaginative reconstruction and interpretation. Evidence is the surviving deposit of an historical event; in order to rediscover the event, the historian must read not only with the analytical eye of the investigator but also with the comprehensive eye of the story-teller. The truth is the product of this double process : understanding what the evidence really says, and understanding how it fits together. But if the product is really to be the truth, controls, once again, are necessary, and here there are two : the asking of right questions, and the application of informed standards of probability.

Right questions means fruitful questions, questions capable of producing answers. They must therefore be geared to what is contained in the matter to be enquired from : the evidence need not by any means supply answers to all the questions the historian would like to ask. Secondly, they must be penetrating; they must really exhaust the possibilities of the evidence. It is no use asking what the views of the peasantry were on the truth of religion as purveyed by the thirteenth-century Church if all we have to go by are statements from the governing sort. However much one may want to know, it is no use asking what people's living standards were at a given time in a given place, if there are absolutely no figures from which an answer could be constructed. Of course, questions that at some time seem unanswerable may become answerable in the hands of the historian who realizes that the evidence can after all be made to yield relevant replies; though this happens often enough and is one of the chief instruments of historical progress, it still leaves much of the past permanently dark. One might, for example, like to know figures for cloth production in England between 1300 and 1500. The only evidence in existence gives an account of such cloth exports as paid duty; beyond that lies an area of obscurity in which cloth smuggled without paying duty (probably a negligible amount) and cloth consumed in the country of production (certainly a large amount) remain forever unassessable. But right questions which seek in the evidence new answers based on real foundations will control the amount of genuine truth that can be added to knowledge. The purpose of a proper research training must therefore include the recognition of the right questions, which means a penetrative analytical approach to the material with a mind alert to every possibility as well as the ready discarding of any questions which turn out to be wrong either because they yield no answer or because they result in no fresh knowledge. The framing of new right questions is the most difficult task the historian can face, and it is therefore reassuring to know that it is a task not often imposed on him. New right questions are occasionally asked by some men of outstanding ability, or by someone who has receptively listened to the practitioners of some other discipline concerned with men; thereafter it takes as a rule more than a generation of historians to apply the new question to the many varieties of human history and societies.[11]

---

[11] In the last few years, 'demographic' questions—vital statistics

But even when the right questions have been asked and the resulting answers subjected to the rigid controls of technical scholarship, there remains one last aid in the search for truth. The answers must be probable; they must agree with what is known to be possible in human experience. This is not to suggest as vague a criterion as may at first sight appear. No one supposes that the historian is entitled to assume for true something that seems to him possible in human terms, and in practice historians tend to be better aware of the danger of arguing by analogy than are sociologists and anthropologists. The point is that the historian comes to this stage of his work at the end of a process which has taken him through the much more independent standards of judgment produced by a rigorous study of the evidence; it is only in the end, when he considers the answers so obtained, that he is entitled to apply the last test: could this have been? And if it clearly could not, he is entitled—indeed, obliged—to reconsider his evidence imaginatively, for he knows that it does not tell him all unless his imagination recreates the circumstances and interdependencies within which the evidence has arisen. The problem most commonly occurs when a sequence of events needs to be explained in which there are gaps. For instance, we know beyond doubt that in the course of the sixteenth century the English Privy Council changed its composition, working habits, and real place in government. We can say with certainty that its

---

of all kinds—have become immensely popular, and rightly so because they analyse some fundamental issues in history. But fashions always get out of hand, and historians working in periods where the evidence to answer such questions simply does not exist should accept their fate with an equanimity born of the recognition that there are other questions capable of being answered.

numbers were at some point reduced by the exclusion of certain men, hitherto members but thereafter described as councillors at large, not privy councillors. We do not know when this happened; no order exists making the change. Two ways of explaining the sequence are therefore possible. The historian may say that the change was carried out on some particular occasion of which we are ignorant. Or he may say that the reorganized body developed gradually, or by stages, from the other. The latter has usually been the alternative chosen, for historians faced with uncertainty, trained to adhere to the known facts and unwilling to stick their necks out, commonly prefer the supposedly safe vagueness of a gradual transition. But apply the criterion of probability, and what happens? Is it possible to envisage a situation in which one part of a group of men is gradually turned from privy councillors into councillors at large, a title hitherto unknown? Could such a change happen without someone telling them that from now on they would be known by this new title, with its reduced functions? And if someone told them, must he not have done so at some particular point in time? In short, is not the second, and usual, explanation simply an evasion of the answer, a vague attempt to cover up ignorance, rendered unconvincing by an imaginative reconstruction of how things must have happened? Known experience and a little thought prove that they could not have happened according to the formula usually used.

Imagination, controlled by learning and scholarship, learning and scholarship rendered meaningful by imagination—those are the tools of enquiry possessed by the historian. He knows that what he is studying is real; he knows that he can never recover all of it and that within his area of recovery the certain, the probable and the speculative will coexist. In short, he knows that the process of historical research and reconstruction will never end, but he is also conscious that this does not render his work unreal or illegitimate. But it is incumbent upon him to reduce the uncertainties to a minimum, whether they are introduced by the deficiencies of the evidence, by the intrusion of the enquiring mind, or—most inescapable of all—by the incomplete relationship between the process of history and the evidence it leaves behind. Therefore he must train himself to his trade and become a man of learning and hardheaded attention to his materials. He must subdue his imagination to the controls which scholarship provides. But he must not destroy it; on the contrary, he must nurture it carefully. The means by which he does this, and the purposes to which he puts it, indispensable enough in the task of research, are also the basis of success in his next task, the writing of history.

III

Writing

If historians thought that their labours involved nothing but research, they would lead easier lives. Honest and thorough research can be exhausting and tedious. But honest and thorough writing will certainly be those things, and the agony of forcing thought into order and pattern should not be despised. The writing of history is no easier than the writing of anything; compared with, say, the writing up of scientific research or even the working out of literary analysis or philosophic argument, it presents difficulties of a peculiarily drastic kind. It may even be thought that the common doubts about the possibility of historical knowledge, which have engaged our attention, sometimes represent unconscious but more justified doubts about the possibility of conveying that knowledge. The more the historian knows, the more he despairs of his ability to tell it, for the sheer complexity of the historical process stands inexorably in the way. At times it seems as though, contrary to reasonable expectations, real understanding and the impossibility of conveying it grew together in steady harmony. Every simple statement immediately seems too simple; every piece of description and explanation calls forth informed doubt in the writer; every clear expression of opinion seems to him to demand qualification, even denial, as he contemplates the variety of experience which he is trying to reduce to order on paper. It does not require the inevitable presence of critics in the wings to teach the honest historian the inadequacy of his own work, and any really learned man among them will be better able than even his dearest enemies to diminish and contradict what he has said.

Small wonder, then, that historians are commonly charged with hedging their bets, with qualifying all they say, with obscuring their subject in a welter of backtrackings and reservations. Life—and therefore history—are like that: they defy the sun-lit clarity and clear-cut road through the wilderness which good writing requires. Indeed, in a very real sense history cannot be correctly written. The processes to be analysed and described occur on a broad front, simultaneously and interconnectedly; writing is a linear development quite unlike the matter to be written about. The human mind is perfectly capable of holding a variety of interacting events, personalities and influences in a well-ordered amalgam; for physical and technical reasons, the pen is vastly less well able to convey this true comprehension to another mind. People talk of straightforward narrative history and seem to think that complexity is introduced by the writer. But what can be straightforward about a narrative which has to hold an infinity of threads in a single skein? What can be simple about a process which demands constant selection and rejection, a permanent multiplicity of choices, an inescapable awareness of the matter left out, the arguments on the other side, and the insufficiency of the activity engaged in? There is a theory that a ready ability to write comes only to the historian equipped with full knowledge. One could wish it were so, but in fact only ignorance makes the writing of history easy. In history, as elsewhere, fools rush in, and the angels may perhaps be forgiven if rather than tread in those treacherous paths they tread upon the fools instead.

Of course, there are ways of escaping the dilemma. One of the more popular is not to write at all, or at least to write very little. Some quite solid reputations have been built in this way. A man known, privately, to be learned can be thought impressively austere and formidable because he cannot bring himself to commit his learning to paper, except perhaps in the occasional small article or the more frequent attack upon others rash enough to write. Except for the reservation that no one who has not offered himself for slaughter has any right to savage others, there need be nothing disreputable in this. Writing is difficult, and to some it can, through no real fault of their own, become impossible. Nevertheless, unless the historian writes he will bury his learning and render his labours sterile : history, to exist, must be written as well as studied. A more respectable way out of the difficulty is to confine one's writing to the manageable, to choose topics which reduce the inherent problem of historical reconstruction to a minimum. Hence the learned monograph, tackling a carefully circumscribed issue usually by way of analysis and description rather than narrative. The account of an institution, the tracing of an idea, the dissection of an economic process, all lend themselves more easily to being presented on paper than does the progress of events in a complex setting of social, economic, political, intellectual or personal circumstances. But more easily does not equal easy; the fundamental difficulties of historical writing remain, as well as the conditions which that writing must fulfil.

Nevertheless, historical writing we must have, or— whether we must or not—shall have. What does it involve? What distinguishes good from bad, adequate from distressing, useful from useless? All historians differ, and the man who does not suppose that he can do at least as well as any other is rare. Any analysis, by a practising historian, of the purposes and qualities of historical writing is bound to be personal and bound to sound self-centred; any advice may well be regarded as arrogant. Yet on the point that there are differences of quality to be found among practitioners the opinions of both historians and non-historians are clear; and while I am aware of the impression which an attempt to define and prescribe must make I cannot feel justified in evading it. In any case, there is a second side to this. The higher the horse mounted by my principles, the happier the critic who can compare them with my practice.

1 Controls

The first question is whether the writing of history, however difficult, is in fact possible. I have tried to show that the historian can discover something fairly described as the truth; it remains to prove that his exposition of the past can claim more than an aesthetic quality and is more than an intellectual game. Is it true that though research may be governed by rules which severely limit the accidental, personal and selective in the search for truth, writing firmly reintroduces them? Up to a point, these doubts were answered in the demonstration that the trained historian works in ways which minimize his intrusion into the story. In the process of learning, he already constructs, and in so far as the first is governed by the integrity imposed by the evidence the second flows from that evidence rather than from the historian's mind. However, it is he who uses the evidence : he chooses, arranges, interprets. As a researcher, he has his defences; we must see whether as a writer he can escape the relativism of personality.

An anonymous reviewer, in the *Times Literary Supplement* of March 24th, 1966, replying to criticism of his article, maintained that historians can write history only by selecting from such facts of the past as past observers have thought it desirable to select for preservation. This double process of screening was inevitable and compelled attention to the historian, not the history he writes : 'this is how all historians work'. Quite possibly he is an historian himself, and it may be that the kind of history he writes is indeed produced in this way, though I find it hard to credit. The historian does not just 'select' facts; he employs them in controlled reconstruction of that past of whose reality he knows them to be evidence. Nor does the critic seem to be well acquainted with the manner in which evidence comes into existence, for that which is deliberately preserved by observers is a drop in the bucket compared with that which is left behind by action and without thought of selection for preservation purposes. Anyone who has ever had occasion to labour among the records of even one law court in even a short period of time will know how inadequate the notion of 'preservation by observers' really is. Nevertheless, limited and somewhat naïve though his view may be, it quite rightly stresses the historian's activity in processing what he uses. Whether he is trying to tell a story or to give an account of past problems, the historian must arrange his comprehension of the past in some intelligent and intelligible pattern of his own, and while this does not permit him to exclude evidence for improper reasons (that it will not fit in or makes his point of view untenable, for instance) he must still make distinctions among the details supplied by his evidence. Some is to be used and some to be discarded as irrelevant, and of the first some elements are treated as more meaningful or useful in explanation than the rest. This is certainly an activity which cannot be reduced to the rigour of the scientific experiment and which accounts in part for the continued and frequent disputes among historians.

But to suppose from this that the historian is in sole control is as false as was the argument, already dealt with, that the historian controls the very existence of his material, and it is false for the same reason. The proper rules of evidence and reason, the instructed processes of historical research, severely limit the historian not only in the interpretation of the remnants of the past but also in his choice of them on grounds of relevancy. The choice is made by seeking answers to questions. The historian wishes to say how the American colonies came to revolt against the mother country, or to account for the spread of cattle-farming across the Argentinian grass lands. He wishes to discern the influence of Aristotle on Christian thinkers in the middle ages or to elucidate the causes of Marlborough's victories over the French. All these are questions one may very properly ask of the evidence—and ask of evidence which can also, as a rule, yield answers to other equally legitimate questions. As the searchlight of the question moves about, it will bring into relief different aspects of one given mountain of evidence. To that extent the selecting mind exercises some control. But if the mind asks questions to which the evidence can supply no answer—if the searchlight points straight upward into the empty sky of pure conjecture—the mind remains a blank. The evidence controls the writer of history and his questions quite as much as he controls it, and its control comes first in time. That is to say, there can be no meaningful (answerable) questions without evidence, but the evidence will still be there, ready to answer questions, though no historian may have been bright enough to ask them. Of course, the whole process is one of interaction and interchange. Reading his material stimulates the historian into questions penetrating enough to give new meaning to the material and lead to further questions pressed upon the historian by the material. The writing and reconstruction of history amount to a dialogue between the historian and his materials. He supplies the intelligence and the organizing ability, but he can interpret and organize only within the limits set by his evidence. And those are the limits created by a true and independent past.

Unfortunately, one common opinion, as expressed in the anonymous letter mentioned before, puts all the weight upon the activating mind and overlooks the activated and activating material. It would seem to derive either from lack of self-awareness in an historian, or from lack of historical experience in a commentator. The notion of the historian formulating his questions and then applying them to whatever he can find, in such a way that the answer is really determined by the question, is unreal.[1] The only questions that the historian can possibly ask before he has started seriously reading his sources are either so large and general ('I wonder what did happen when the American colonies revolted') as to leave the answer quite open, or so particular to the process of research ('I wonder what evidence there is concerning this or that') as to submit him at once to the

[1] I do not deny that some things that pass for historical writing may have been done in this way, but I am concerned with history, not with propaganda or fiction.

discipline of his training. When the work has started the questions will, of course, continue to come, but they will continually arise out of the work, not be sovereignly imposed upon it. One can speak only from experience; this is not only mine alone but of those also with whose work I have had first-hand acquaintance. The theories, for instance, concerning Tudor government which I have proposed and which have met with a good deal of argument and criticism, came to my mind not (as some of my critics would have it) because mine was a naturally authoritarian mind looking for virtue in rulers, but because the evidence called them forth. When I started on that evidence, my mind was as well stocked with received notions as a solid course of reading other people's writings could make it; it was the real evidence of the past which destroyed those notions and replaced them with fresh thinking. I may have misinterpreted the evidence, but I did not adjust it to my questions and preconceptions.

Thus, whatever may be argued in the abstract, and remembering that on top of his reconstruction the historian will express opinions which are a great deal more personal than the intellectual solution of problems, the selection and control employed by the historian are themselves guided and controlled to a very high degree by the materials to which he applies his treatment. It is, however, important to note that in one respect the materials are a great deal less concrete than has so far been alleged. That the evidence of the past can change shape and meaning under the historian's questing eye has already been admitted, and all that was said in the preceding chapter was designed to show how proper observance of the rules will limit the extravagances of such changes. What is less easily reduced to approximate certainty is the evidence that is not there. Especially for ages of which little has survived, the student depends not only on extant material but also on that which is missing but must have existed—the gaps in the text, the lost books known to have been written, the additional documents unquestionably produced by a known administrative process but no longer there. Historical writing involves both learning and imagination, both knowing what exists and understanding the complexity of the missing materials within which it exists. Evidence invariably grows in the process of interpretation beyond the mere surface appearance which it might continue to present to the layman. But it can grow only within the rigorous terms set by the rules of evidence and probability, not laws of nature but guiding lines rendered strict enough by training and insight to reduce the variable, once again, within pretty narrow limits.

The exercise of this kind of imagination can run all the way from the incontrovertible demonstration to the highly problematic guess. Certainly, the fact that historians conjecture and imagine beyond what they hold in the hand, and that they are right to do so, will keep argument and controversy alive; but argument and controversy are themselves controlled by the historian's principles of learning. (Sometimes they are controlled by malice and envy, but we are concerned with the real thing only.) The whole process of interpretation and analysis, already described, involves exercises of personal thought which reduce the scientific accuracy, even the agreed substance, of the historian's work. Those who would put all the emphasis on these variant factors would seem to me to place their bets on the wrong horse. A mind trained in the double technicalities of historical research—precise learning and imaginative understanding—will eliminate so much of the merely haphazard that the accuracy rather than the uncertainty of his work will strike the eye first. Some historical writing is simply and obviously right, some is a good deal more likely to be correct than not, some is pretty doubtful, some even good work may be wild. But the very practice of historical writing, and the occurrence of historical controversy, demonstrate that historians think themselves capable of reproducing the truth, whether they have worked out the grounds of this belief or not; and whether they are right or wrong—good historians or indifferent—they really have this conviction because they have been through the mill of learned investigation and reconstruction.

There is no final end to the study of history; the true and complete past can never be described because not enough of it survives and because what survives must be interpreted by human minds. All problems except the simplest, and sometimes so simple a point as a date or place, continue to be open to argument and doubt. Yet the freedom of exploration which this guarantees is firmly circumscribed by the reality of the past, independent of any observer, and by the tested practices which take the observer, with all his personal quirks and human imperfection, towards that reality. The historian's freedom is responsible, and in his case as in others responsibility confines rather than liberates. The study of historians can be very interesting, and a knowledge of the writer usually has something to contribute to an understanding of his work; but the study of history remains valid in itself, and a writer's contribution to knowledge stands apart from the mind he has brought to his labours.

2 Patterns and Bias

When it comes to transferring understanding to paper, the historian faces new difficulties which, in the eyes of some, may deprive him of any right to claim authority. The practical difficulties of writing—of rendering in convincing words what may be perfectly plain to the mind—are perhaps especially large in so complex an intellectual game as the writing of history. However, as has already been said, these can be overcome by art and skill, based on thought. Two more inherent obstacles resist removal. One is created by the need to make sense of things; the other by the fact that the mind which makes sense of things is not a photographic plate, blank until exposed to the light cast by the evidence.

Since historical reconstruction is a rational process, only justified and indeed possible if it involves the human reason, what we call history is the mess we call life reduced to some order, pattern and possibly purpose. This is not to say that the historian needs necessarily to see a 'larger' purpose at work in the fates of generations— God, or inevitability, or even personified History itself. I have already ruled out this prophet's ambition as irrelevant to a man's capacity as historian. The point is rather that whatever piece of the past the historian reconstructs must, to be present to the mind, achieve a shape of beginning and end, of cause and effect, of meaning and intent. If, as he ought to be, the historian is in addition an artist, a man wishing to create (in words) a thing of interest and beauty, the constructive element in the process can become overpowering; and if political motives supervene it becomes really dangerous. Take a very well known case, the seventeenth-century revolutions in England. The almost universal notion that that age was one in which everything in society underwent revolutionary experiences seems supported by the evidence of events—civil war, a king killed, revolutionary governments, dispossessions. The aesthetic pattern also demands, and gets, the arrangement of a true drama, a conflict between opposing truths and rights fought out at a high level of passion and tragic beauty. On top of that, the outcome produced the politically weighty interpretation of a struggle for liberty and rights, very properly won. Thus everything combined to create a very durable pattern for that century which no historian has yet tried to recast, though many have taken important parts away or quite refurbished others. The axiom that this was a 'century of revolutions' is no longer tested, it seems so obvious; and in turn it produces new 'revolutions', as for instance ingenious if implausible links between social rebellion and intellectual reorientation.[2] Yet an attempt to free the mind from the pressures of a conventional pattern, to absorb the results of research, and to think about the whole age afresh, suggests that the pattern is at the very least too simple, possibly quite wrong, and that the appearance of revolutionary changes has been allowed, for one reason and another, to hide the curious absence of really meaningful change in society, politics, or the distribution of wealth.[3]

[2] The most extreme manifestation of this is Christopher Hill's *Intellectual Origins of the Puritan Revolution* (Oxford, 1965) which argues that Puritanism and an interest in the new natural science are facets of the same state of mind. The evidence will not support this view which really springs from the deep conviction with which a certain historical pattern is believed in (cf. *Past and Present*, no. 31, 104ff.; 32, 110ff.; *History and Theory*, v. 61ff.)

[3] Taking into account our new knowledge of the surrounding centuries, and deliberately applying a possibly too sceptical

Pattern-making cannot be avoided; interpretation forms the historian's proper and necessary task. To make it possible to understand an historical event or phenomenon means to show how its pieces fitted together. Meaningful interconnection in the particular, illuminating generalization beyond the individual case—these are the marks that distinguish the inspired and inspiring historian from the hack. Anyone who reads a work of history, whether he be a professional colleague or not, should derive from it some mental elevation, the elevation which comes from seeing reason at work in ordering the seemingly chaotic. But in this activity, of course, the historian must intrude or even impose himself; what he is, will come out very strongly. Impersonal history is dead, whether the impersonality applies to the writer or to his matter. Certainly, this has its dangers. The most insidious consists of that preference for the rational which has already been discussed. Discovering the pattern in history, making sense of it, depends on the application of reason, and it is always possible that no such rational thinking took place in the actual fashioning of the event described. This is a danger that cannot be escaped. One can allow for the irrational, emotional, even insane elements in history, but even in allowing for them and fitting them into the explanation one uses reason and consequently may distort or misrepresent. However, this is not only inevitable but also insignificant: as I said earlier, reason does in measure work in men's lives, and on balance actions and motives are much more commonly explained correctly on the assumption that some form of thinking has taken place, rather than

attitude, I have argued a case for treating the century as markedly less than revolutionary, in *Annali della Fondazione Italiana per la Storia Amministrativa*, ii. 759ff.

that they welled up out of some unconscious which defies analysis.

Then there is the danger of overdoing the pattern-making. Since the historian is fully entitled to construct the probable from his well-founded knowledge, using both his understanding of the humanly possible and his living comprehension of the age studied (and distinguishing honestly between knowledge and conjecture), he will commonly be tempted to make sense everywhere. But a good many things in life, and therefore in history, are truly extraneous to other things, do not in fact belong with them or play upon them. Isolated events, lost thoughts, false starts, eremitical existences do occur. The insufficiency of the evidence bars too universal a view. Temperaments differ : some historians like to see 'profound significance' (usually of a morally based kind) at every turn; others take a delight in discovering only the commonplace or petty or accidental. The wise historian will be aware of his quirks and will temper both his imagination and his cunning with the caution born of active research. Above all, he will remember that sometimes he simply does not know or cannot explain or cannot fit in. He does not have to love the imperfections of his labours, but he had better resign himself to living with them.

There is a particular case of this general problem which deserves mention even though it has been discussed often enough before. Perhaps the historian's most difficult handicap—much worse than any mere prejudice—lies in his inevitable hindsight. It is true enough that only knowledge of what came after makes him into an historian at all, but (as is so often the case with the little gifts of the gods) that with which he can least dispense also most subtly corrupts him. Since we know how things worked out, we are twice tempted to suppose that they were bound to work out in this way, and to consider the known outcome to be in some way 'right'. The first frees the historian of his basic duty to explain : if what happened was inevitable no thought is required in understanding it. The second makes him into a tedious defender of accomplished fact and leads him to consider the past only in the light of the present, the notorious weakness already denounced. These are genuine errors to beware of. The historian must not simply assume rightness in a cause which triumphed and error in one that was defeated. He may still express views, even moral judgments, but not on the mere grounds of survival and disappearance, of victory and defeat. His right posture will be inside the event, though as a being exceptionally gifted, for purposes of explanation, with knowledge of what came next. And in seeing things in shape and order, he must avoid like the plague any conviction that the course of events was necessary or determined. Whether all things seem to him to work inevitably to a new heaven or tread a path of doom, the ready determinist is a bore who uses criteria of explanation that he cannot derive from the materials or techniques of history. It is not these that enable him to make the equation 'what is was bound to be', but his faith which encourages him to ignore the multifarious and particular. That certain events were clearly and perhaps predictably the consequence of others is a conclusion at which the historian may at best arrive at the end of his studies and with an appreciation that their turn could not have been predicted at the time with any certainty. Hindsight is a help, an enlargement of the understanding, not a substitute for argument and empathy.

This business of shaping the pattern and the explanation is beset, it seems, by serious philosophical problems involving the very question whether historical explanation (deducing consequences from disparate facts) is possible at all. This need not concern us, except to note that what troubles the logician and the philosopher seems least to worry those even amongst them who have had some experience of what working among the relics of the past means. From the point of view of understanding the past, the many learned discussions concerning the sense in which historians explain it are quite remarkably barren and irrelevant. When it comes to explanation, it is a more serious matter that the historian may evade the task by using some of the short-hand terms with which convention has equipped him. A strange conviction dictates that a pattern becomes the more intellectually respectable the more it is expressed in abstract language. The concept of cause being under a cloud (because it used to be employed too crudely) historians have for a time been hunting for a substitute. Wherever one turns in history to-day, one runs head-on into factors. There no longer are any causes of the Reformation; instead there are factors that made it possible. This is to go from the tolerably dubious to the quite abominable. A cause is something real : people do things in order to produce results. A factor—outside mathematics and trading stations and Scottish estates— is a meaningless piece of tired jargon. Events are not the product of simple causes but of complex situations in which a variety of people and circumstances participates, but this does not mean that they are produced by factors. A word to be forgotten.[4]

---

[4] Sometimes 'factor' is used—because it sounds more scientific?— even in place of poor old 'fact': 'A major factor retarding the deterioration of Anglo-American relations was the dispute that called James Monroe to Madrid' (Bradford Perkins, *The First Rapprochement,* Princeton, 1955, 177). For some wise words on this nonsense see J. H. Hexter, *Reappraisals in History,* 195ff.

This fault is probably only verbal. More serious trouble arises for the historian for whom events take place in a setting of the purely impersonal. Ever since economics started impinging on historians we have heard of forces; since statistics were added to their equipment, we have met trends. That both these concepts are ugly and often dull may be no good reason for avoiding them; but what of their meaning? Do the 'forces' so readily resorted to by some historians have any reality? The pressures of the market, the influence of inflation, even the mental climate of an age, are not without independent and significant existence. Trends, too, do exist : that is to say, it is possible to extract from a sequence of facts a general movement or a general condition which suggests direction, upwards, downwards, or see-saw. It would be quite improper to condemn every use of these or similar words, every reference to abstractions from human activity. The trouble arises when they are used improperly, when forces are made to act without agents, and trends—statistical definitions of a movement in events—are themselves made to act. Abstractions describe; they must not be personified into activators. That there was a trend to this or that is something the historian may say, though as a rule he will do well to find a better choice of words. That a trend ever decided or did anything is, given the real meaning of the word, palpable nonsense, and people cannot therefore ever be said to have done, said or suffered anything because of a trend.

All this accumulation of factors, forces and trends— others will be able to add their own dislikes to the list—reflects a form of mental indolence. In briefly summing things up to himself, the historian may employ such terms because it saves time to do so, because it may define main lines of the pattern for him, and because he is (or should be) carefully aware of the inadequacies of such language. In explaining things to others, he has little right to use them because then they only represent one of two things: his inability to think clearly, or his ignorance. To use these evasions by way of explanation is to explain nothing and to reveal one's failure to understand. It is a more subtle form of that sort of mysticism which uses unfilled concepts like national characteristics or the spirit of the age as though they held a meaning precise enough to explain phenomena. There is a perfectly simple cure for these besetting sins of vaporous abstraction. History does not exist without people, and whatever is described happens through and to people. Therefore let us talk about people, by all means imposing categories on them and abstracting generalizations from them, but not about large miasmic clouds like forces or busy little gnomes like trends.

There remains the question of bias in the historian, an ancient topic of debate and a somewhat tired one. To me, the understandable reaction against claims to 'ultimate history', free of all personal preconceptions, has gone too far. No one now supposes that what the historian is in himself does not affect his writing, but (as we have seen) most people who express themselves on this point seem a little too ready to see the historian and forget the history. This attitude ranges from the sort of view held by the anonymous reviewer already cited to the growing habit, especially strong in American universities, of studying problems through the contrasting opinions of selected writers rather than from the evidence. Historiography has its uses, as an auxiliary science as well as a parlour game, but when it takes the place of history it arrogates to itself a position it is unfitted to fill.[5] That

[5] See below, p. 192.

every generation rewrites history from its own point of view, and that every historian worth reading has a mind filled with attitudes of his own, are common-places, largely true, which need not be laboured any further. Yet in all this preoccupation with the historian, people do seem to fail to notice how the supposed products of bias and preoccupation come to be the common property of all, including those most deter-mined to reveal the bias and preconceptions that went to the making of them.

When Sir Lewis Namier, a man rather good at making enemies, exploded his bomb in 1929, he claimed to be doing nothing but look at the evidence.[6] He showed that the conventional categories in which eighteenth-century political history had been discussed did not rest upon the facts of the past. Because he could be said to be a tory delighting in combating whig views, resistance could evade the issue, and it took some fifteen years for his 'revolution' to penetrate into the general accounts. This triumph of conservatism incidentally shows that not every generation always re-writes history in terms suitable to itself. Then, after 1945, Namier's views became embalmed in a general adulation from which few dissented, until now, after his death, the protests and revisions come thick and fast. As is usual, the protests seem often to assail irrelevancies or views he did not hold, but what matters is that even those who most object to the Namierite explanation of English politics talk entirely in terms first established by

[6] *The Structure of Politics at the Accession of George III*, a collection of essays demonstrating the real purposes and relation-ships in eighteenth-century politics and attacking the notion of organized party which had hitherto underlain all discussions of that time. Namier did not make acceptance easier by failing to provide an alternative coherent structure for the one which he removed.

him.[7] No one now would dream of interpreting the
England of the unreformed Parliament in the way
universal before Namier wrote. Even those who still
want to use the terms whig and tory, or who would
give a higher place than Namier did to the political ideas
and convictions held by eighteenth-century politicians,
have completely absorbed his essential demonstration
of the parliamentary scene. It may be that Namier's own
personality—his own attitude to politics or his anti-
liberal bias—helped him to break out of a conventional
framework, but what made his revision so solid that it
has now become, even to opponents, the new conventional framework was his firm foundation of scholarship. He was studying history—trying to find out—not
promoting a personal point of view, or merely (as
some do) wishing to create a stir by being different.

Namier's case shows the real place of bias, of the
historian's personality, in the business of writing history.
It enables him to look afresh at the facts of the past. If
it goes further, it commonly defeats its purpose. This is
as true of unconscious bias as of conscious. The historian
who deliberately sets out to prove a case agreeable to
his own prejudices is no real problem as an historian,
though like any propagandist he can be dangerous on
a wider stage. Notoriously, the nationalist convictions
of most nineteenth-century German historians helped
to indoctrinate generations with misleading and sometimes pernicious beliefs about the past, and unlike most
notorious things this one contains some truth. The

[7] This is especially true of the more serious writers, e.g. H.
Butterfield in *George III and the Historians* (London, 1957). For a
fine example of silly criticism, allegedly employing the tools of
political science but in fact displaying only obscurantism and
self-advertisement, see Harvey C. Mansfield, 'Sir Lewis Namier
Re-Considered', *Journal of British Studies*, ii. 28ff.

falsely glamorous view of the Stuart monarchy, and
the obscurely apologetic air concerning the Reformation,
which one still finds among a good many people who
read history of a sort, owe less to the true revisions of
an older bias made by historians than to the falsehoods
purveyed by Cardinal Gasquet and Hilaire Belloc. The
real study and understanding of history have been
virtually unaffected by such things. As long as discussion
continues, and especially as long as the issues discussed
are alive, the obvious or hidden preferences of the historian will intervene but are quickly discovered and
allowed for; what remains are the positive products of
scholarship, originally often directed in its search by
some bias, products which endure only if thanks to
scholarship they have risen above the mere expression of
prejudice. This is not to deny that prejudiced views are
sometimes difficult to combat (the influence of so-called
left wing attitudes in English economic history is a fair
example); misleading interpretations can have a long
life. Constant vigilance is needed, both towards others
and, what is much more difficult, towards oneself. But
the corrective exists, in the proper training of the professional historian.

Historians' personalities and private views are a fact of
life, like the weather; and like the weather they are
not really worth worrying about as much as in practice
they are worried over. They cannot be eliminated, nor
should they be. The historian who thinks that he has
removed himself from his work is almost certainly
mistaken; what in fact he is likely to have proved is
the possession of a colourless personality which renders
his work not sovereignly impartial but merely dull. But
though dullness is no virtue, neither is self-conscious
flamboyance. The historian need not try either to

eliminate or to intrude himself; let him stick to the writing of history and forget the importance of his psyche. It will be there all right and will no doubt be served by his labours, but really it matters less to the result than critics lament or friends acclaim, and it matters a great deal less than does his intellect.

3 Style

History, then, can be written; historians pursue a humanly possible task. Indeed, for purposes of discussion, history does not exist until it has been reconstructed and written down by the historian. It lives by the word, and the historian's first concern must be to respect and regard words. Styles and methods of expression differ and there is room for many of them in the capacious mansions of historical writing. However, there is room only for those that fulfil the conditions set by the fact that no one writes except to be read. It is in this sense that history is an art. No matter how scientific the process of research may be, that of presentation requires skills of exposition, explanation and persuasion which all turn upon the right use of words. I am far from supposing that a single manner is appropriate to all forms of historical writing, or even to any single form of it, and I know of no worse prescription than that which advises the beginner to form his style upon some eminent model. What the writer is, both as a man and as an historian, will appear in the style of his writing. This is not to say that one cannot learn from others, both from their excellences and their mistakes, but one cannot copy the style of a Macaulay, a Gibbon, or a Maitland except to write pastiche, which in history is not worth the effort. However, no matter what writing comes naturally to the historian, it must be readable and may be judged by that standard.

Readability is not the same thing as meretriciousness. Some widely read historians, criticized by the less successful, come to believe that they are blamed for lack of scholarship when the hidden charge is that they attract readers. At one time there was something in this complaint, and in some parts of the world there still is. In the earlier part of this century, a good many scholars seem to have thought that the more readable their colleagues were the less they merited consideration. Difficult things, 'real problems', could not be dealt with in lucid or attractive language but required obscure technical terms and a style which reflected the agonizing processes of thought that had gone into their analysis. Any historian who expressed himself well and showed some respect for the remarkable possibilities of the English language was automatically assumed to have achieved ease of expression by sliding over the difficulties of the matter. Perhaps he was not even aware of them; perhaps he had deliberately sacrificed depth and accuracy to his ambition to become a publisher's dream; it was hard to say which failing deserved the more severe censure. The work of so popular an historian as G. M. Trevelyan gave some substance to this embittered attitude: he, and some others, too often achieved literary distinction by an easy saunter around any problem of intellectual gravity and by superficial methods of explanation which left the serious and involved student gasping. Only Maitland was free from this censure, and what made him exceptional was his manifest willingness to tackle the most recondite and technical problems without any concession to the reader's supposed inability to grasp them, yet in language so splendidly lucid that he invariably did grasp them.

In those years, it seems to have been the fashion to think that only a particularly austere and even repulsive style of writing could entitle the historian to the name of scholar, and some men appeared to reserve a special vocabulary and syntax for the occasions on which they wished to claim that distinction. That eminent medievalist, James Tait, who taught at the University of Manchester for nearly forty years, is reported by those who heard him to have been a singularly lucid and brilliant lecturer. No trace of this comes through in his writing which is obscure and painful; his one major work, a study of *The Medieval English Borough*, is quite as tiresome to read as (to judge from the length of time it took to appear) it was to produce. That very competent scholar, A. F. Pollard, wrote biographies which all could read and many read with pleasure; but when he turned his hand to a learned article, fluency turned to a stammer and proper precision to pernickety obscurity. Scholars took pride in writing only for other scholars. This should not have absolved them from the demands of art, but since those others could not escape reading what was offered, the manner of presentation was at best thought a point of little importance. The attitude extended, however, beyond the needs of scholars. A. W. Ward, who dominated the *Cambridge Modern History* after Acton's death and edited the *Cambridge History of British Foreign Policy* in the 1920's, was one of the most influential men in the profession. Allegedly an interesting talker, he wrote without colour and drained the colour from others, too. On one occasion he explained the difficulties he had with a contributor's chapter by saying that 'it's a bit lively'.[8] There, from the mouth of one who at Manchester had taught not only history but also English language and literature, spoke the voice of the profession. The learned dullness of those histories stands as a monument to a mistaken puritanism. This gild attitude to scholarship promoted real delight in involution, in being comprehensible only to what were sometimes called one's peers. The stumbling solemnity that often hung about that attitude reflected a measure of uncertainty about the activity engaged in : mumbo-jumbo, private language, the barriers of technicality are not so much intended to keep the mob out as to pretend that there is something of value inside the zareba. Intellectual enterprise which prefers to hide behind obscurity and mere clumsiness cannot be very sure of itself or its own ultimate worth.[9] Even justified contempt for the intellectual softness of many popular writers does not excuse this attitude. The historian must not always write just for a small circle of his fellows; the way to combat bad popular history is to write good popular history, not to retreat from the world.

In England this rather tiresome pose has been in retreat for the past twenty years. It is not dead, any more than helpless bad writing is dead, nor has the determination to write so as to be read always led to happy results. One or two historians have publicly replied to valid scholarly criticism of their works by citing their sales charts. Others, less innocent, may be less candid but are too often willing to adjust to the market. Yet neither the desire to shock nor the desire to pander to

[8] Cf. S. C. Roberts, *Adventures with Authors* (Cambridge, 1966), 112-113.
[9] In this respect sociologists have now taken over from the historians. They are welcome to that part of the inheritance, at any rate.

modest understanding are very good fairies to attend at the production of historical research. However, the general level of historical writing has clearly risen. Not only has the expansion of higher education called forth an increasing number of well-presented historical accounts; not only is there something of a boom in history for the intelligent layman, a fair amount of it being 'real' history; but it is, at least, my impression that those expressions of scholarship which can never have a wide audience are to-day less hedged about by poor, obscure or lifeless writing than once they were. In such respects, America has still to follow suit. There one still encounters the old double standard; men who express themselves very prettily in conversation or, occasionally, on the platform, pull out some special dictionary of polysyllabic jargon when they come to write, in the conviction that the fraternity will not otherwise recognize them as scholars. The rank growth and the high repute of the social sciences seem to overwhelm too many American historians with a desire to sound learned. Of course, generalizations of this order carry with them any number of exceptions, but on the whole it looks as though English historians are now better able to fulfil the claims of history as an art, without losing their scholarly rigour and the right to scholarly regard, than are those of America, or for that matter those of Germany. At least, one no longer hears a man decried just because he writes well.

But signs of improvement do not equal the millennium, nor is deliberate art used to disguise an inferior product the same thing as good writing. Unless the substance is good, the appearance, painted even an inch thick, will not please. However, we cannot spare time here for skilful writing pretending to be good history. We are concerned only with history sufficiently good to have the compliment of good writing paid to it. And it has to be admitted that much of what appears as the result of genuine labours and real thought is still hidden in dull and bad writing. What makes writing dull and bad? Rising high above all other faults is lack of life which results from an unwillingness to think and a readiness to repeat other people's thoughts parrot-fashion. There is not much to be done about this by anyone except the writer himself : he alone can distil the necessary elixir from his own brain and bones. But there are two main technical pitfalls on which it is worth offering advice : the use of jargon in place of real words, and incompetence in the use of real words themselves.

One must distinguish between jargon and technical terms. No one can, and no one should, discuss medieval law without such words as dower or novel disseisin, the Reformation without referring to justification by faith alone or the spiritual presence in the eucharist, the growth of industrial economies without admitting profit margins and interest rates to his discourse. History necessarily comprehends many studies and disciplines that are highly technical in themselves and must therefore have a technical vocabulary. But history is not itself a technical study in this sense, which is why those bewitched by the spurious precision and the law-discovering unrealities of the so-called social sciences dislike and despise it. It should explain itself in terms accessible to all men, not to experts only, and if it is obliged to use technical terms, because in the circumstances they are the right ones, it must both understand and explain them. What is not permitted to the historian is the use of technical terms borrowed for no specific reason, used to suggest a non-existent profundity or a spurious scientific framework, and manifestly not expanded in terms of plain language. This rule unhappily eliminates those usefully vague metaphors taken from biology—the institutions that 'evolve', the bodies of opinion that 'mature'.[10] It particularly inhibits recent developments in social history where phrases like class struggle, social mobility, demographic curve and the like are bandied about without being given the real content that historical method and understanding require.[11] It even invalidates such seemingly harmless evasions of the historian's task to explain as the use of words like 'inevitable' or 'predetermined', for words like these, at home in logic and theology, have no accurate meaning in a study which at best can say that *y* was the result of *x*, never that only *y* could have been the result of *x*.

The rule which distinguishes technical terms from jargon is simple enough in theory though a good deal more difficult to apply in practice. Technical terms become jargon when they are used out of the context in which they are technical, or when they are used as substitutes for an explanation. The test by which jargon can most commonly be detected is this: take a piece of writing full of seemingly weighty phrases and try to transcribe it into English. If it then appears as a genuine argument, all is well. If the transcript produces tautology or nonsense, you have been exposed to jargon.

Strictures of this sort are unacceptable unless they are backed by examples, but here to give examples is manifestly to add to one's list of enemies. Still, the risk

[10] A. F. Pollard called one of his books *The Evolution of Parliament*; from one species into another, by a process of natural selection preserving or losing genetically determined characteristics? And what else, if not that? Biological metaphors are the devil: what are we to think of the writer who allowed 'a small misstatement [to] breed a big misconception' (G. R. Elton in *Eng. Hist. Rev.* lxvi, 1951, 508, n.1)?

[11] I.e., even the rules of good writing dispose of Marxist history, a marvellous repository of jargon.

must be run. I will take a book which, I believe, contains some valuable insights and analysis, but which I also believe is marred by the faith in jargon that destroys style: C. H. and K. George's *The Protestant Mind of the English Reformation* (Princeton, 1961). On p. 4 we read:

> Theology constituted the fundamental intellectuality of the seventeenth-century *Weltanschauung*.

Weltanschauung means an intellectual view of life; therefore this sentence says that in the seventeenth century theology formed the intellectual foundation of the fundamental intellectual attitudes of the time. Tautology. On p. 248:

> There is, in fact, a curious vein of social atavism in the clerical commentary on the mores of the aristocracy.

This (to judge from the context) is intended to say that the authors are surprised to find preachers nostalgically praising chivalric virtues, later called, naturally enough in this pompous language, 'prowess at arms and *gloire*'. The surprise, in fact, rests on preconceived notions which the evidence shows to be false; the jargon could serve to disguise the poverty of the thought and the lack of historical discernment. On p. 396 they say:

> In this disproportion between institution and belief— the somewhat schizoid quality of the English Church —there undoubtedly exists a tension-producing capacity which is fully exemplified in the presbyterian agitation.

Translated, this reads (if I have got it right): 'because the Church of England claimed general authority as an institution but permitted variety of belief, an extreme attack on it as an institution, namely presbyterianism, could be promoted from within it'. Here we have both tautology and the trite, made to appear portentously significant by misapplied technical terms, schizoid and tension-producing. The authors are not ascribing the phenomenon they discuss to the vagaries of group or individual psychology but to aspects of organization. Those terms, though deplorably ugly, have their place in psychology; there is no occasion for them here.

These examples, intentionally taken from a work of real merit, may suffice to explain the issue. *Weltanschauung*, atavism, schizoid are all quite proper and possibly useful terms in their technical meaning. This does not entitle the historian to use them out of their technical context or by way of avoiding thought. If he does, he will produce obscurity masquerading as profundity, emptiness pretending to be significance.

But technical terms are not the only ones to get misused; far too often one finds careful and competent historians paying too little heed to the manner in which they employ the ordinary language. The conventional rules of style are no less weighty for being familiar : say exactly what you mean, no more and no less; prefer the concrete to the abstract, the active to the passive mood, directness to circumlocution; attend to the rules of grammar and syntax. Everybody will have his pet hates; mine include pendant participles ('being given to dubious behaviour, the divine wrath struck down Sodom and Gomorrha . . .') and the confusion of 'who' and 'whom'. Again, the rule ought to be simple : make sure that you have said exactly what you meant to say, observing the accepted usages and canons of the English language. However, everybody who has to read a lot of history knows how readily even respectable writers fall

into clumsiness and muddle, sometimes to the point
of real obscurity. The cause may be only tiredness or
an inadequate training, or it may be an incurably bad
ear, but the results are distressing. A recent article
quoted, apparently with approval, a short passage from
a doctoral dissertation which will illustrate the point.
Dissertations do not need to be masterpieces of writing;
indeed, dullness is probably unavoidable in a work
which is required to spell out everything and comes
from a beginner in the craft. On the other hand, the
beginner should also from the first be trained to write
reasonably well and clearly; no more than any other
kind of historian should he be allowed to commit
solecisms or employ bad grammar to produce ambiguity.

The passage in question reads:

> Collective references or designations of political align-
> ments were usually made with regard to the respective
> sides of the House, to administration and opposition,
> and, less frequently, to the majority and the minority.
> Little use was made of the terms whig and tory. On
> infrequent occasions a member might assert he was
> expounding whig doctrines: never did any claim to
> be a tory, but the term was sometimes used as a
> method of reproach.

This perpetrates more minor howlers than one would
suppose possible in a few lines. It avoids the clarity
of directness with determined success, is grammatically
obscure, and misuses words. The first sentence has to be
read more than once to discover its meaning, which
turns out to be that certain expressions were commonly
used to describe the two sides of the House of Commons.
'On infrequent occasions' is a flabby circumlocution, and
the omission of 'that' after 'assert' throws out the rhythm

of the sentence. 'Never did any claim' is an unsuccessful attempt at brightening the writing which adds ambiguity: one stumbles over 'any' for an appreciable moment before one is sure that the word belongs to 'member' and not to 'claim'. Finally, a term cannot become a method. The passage could be rewritten as follows:

> When men wished to give collective names or descriptions of political alignment to the two sides of the House, they usually spoke of administration and opposition, more rarely of the majority and the minority. They almost never used the words whig and tory. Very occasionally a member might assert that he was expounding whig doctrines; none ever claimed to be a tory, though the term was sometimes used by way of reproach.

This is a plain statement of fact, interesting in the context of the question posed; it needs no 'fine' writing, but that does not mean that the writing can be forgiven for being slipshod, tired and unrevised.

How, then, can one avoid these far from uncommon faults? Not all history can be written vividly and with the drive of verbal passion; the subject matter may not permit it. Nevertheless, all historical writing should approach the ideal in two respects: no one should ever write a sentence which he has not personally thought through, and one should always remember that what is said did actually happen. The historian who says things not just because others have said them before him but because he has re-thought each point or issue afresh will not, in most cases, come up with a new answer; but it will be *his* answer, assimilated in *his* mind, expressed in *his* words, and it will thereby renew its freshness. And the historian who remembers that his material has a true life, a past life of its own, that the things he discusses happened to and through live people, should have gone a long way towards giving vitality to his writing. He who thinks all the time and is thoroughly aware cannot go to sleep; by the same token, he will not inflict sleep on others.[12]

4 Audience

The writer of history wishes others to read the history he writes. Does this mean that in writing he should keep his audience constantly in mind? This would certainly seem to be the usual advice. Books should differ with the people to whom they are addressed. One writes in one way for schoolboys, in another for one's colleagues, in yet a third for those 'general readers' whose avid desire for agreeable history it is the ambition of authors and publishers to satisfy. On the face of it, this sounds like a counsel of sense; yet I believe it to be both wrong-headed and rather pernicious. It leads to a subtle arrogance in the writer and to that gild-spirit which at times bids fair to drive the life from the work of the profession. What right has anyone to say, 'this is too much for little minds; this I must reserve for others as able, as gifted, as profound as myself'? And is it any wonder that a man convinced that he is dealing in mysteries too deep for the generality will in the end just tend that feeble flame in the inner sanctuary, forget the world, and live in the sinful pride of the initiate?

[12] Another example: 'This organizational growth, territorially fragmented if denominationally uniform' (G. R. Elton, *Reformation Europe*, London, 1963, 57)—horribly ugly and burdened with a bogus metaphor ('growth') and a false 'if'.

Whether it is worse for the historian to retreat into the exclusiveness of the sect or to proclaim his sectarian arrogance by a vast condescension in writing for the multitude may be a moot point; speaking for myself, I can respect austerity, but I know nothing worse than the sort of book which on every page announces that of course these matters are very difficult for the reader and (if not ostentatiously omitted) had better be explained in simple (and inaccurate) language, by means of so-called modern parallels, by references to the supposed commonplace concerns of the reader, by images and metaphors and slang (usually slang just out of date) supposedly current in the world in which history has to make its way against a main preoccupation with mundane things.[18] I can feel regretful respect for the historian who decides that the world has nothing to do with him and that he will wear his hairshirt exclusively in the pages of the *English Historical Review*; but I feel much less happy about one who, mounting the pulpit, addresses his inferiors in terms suitable for them. No audience, in any case, will respond favourably to being treated as unintelligent; why should it? It is, obviously, the task of the practitioner to explain the difficult things, not to push them considerately out of sight, and there must always be a suspicion that any historian who supposes that he has things to tell which only the expert can understand has not yet himself succeeded in understanding them.

There is really no need for these coy and displeasing

[18] A common fault is coyness, often expressed in long words: 'Elizabeth showed herself her father's daughter by abandoning affairs of state in favour of a round of amusements mixed with dalliance' (G. R. Elton, *England under the Tudors*, London, 1955, 324). The cliché is not redeemed by being accurate enough in point of fact.

attitudes. One can, in such matters, speak only from personal experience, and I must say that in writing and lecturing I endeavour to give no thought to the supposedly differing needs and standards of readers or listeners. Of course, I want to explain myself to them, but my concern has been to expound what I believe to be the truth, or at least what I believe to be the real problems, in the language appropriate to the subject, not perhaps to the audience. Regard your audience as intelligent though possibly uninstructed, and they will indeed prove intelligent and (one hopes) depart better instructed. No problem of historical study that I have come across, in my own work or that of others, has seemed to me incapable of being explained with full clarity to any person of reasonable intelligence, and no person of insufficient intelligence will anyhow be in the way of reading or hearing historical analysis and description. If the historian has really explained things to himself, he can explain them to others; and nothing whatsoever justifies him in supposing that the others need a different treatment, a different language, a lower intensity of thought than himself. In all writing, three dignities must be observed : the dignity of the historian who must play neither the high priest nor the clown, the dignity of the audience who must actively and intelligently cooperate, and above all the dignity of the matter treated. This is no call for pomposity; there has to be respect for the rights of all involved without superior condescension, deliberate simplification, or ostentatious pity. Of course, the type of audience addressed may determine the length and detail of the explanation; it may affect the amount of technical language used. But there can be no reason for it to determine the amount of technical matter or the degree to which the problems receive explanation.

However, historical writings manifestly differ in some quite fundamental ways—in length, in subject matter, in structure and purpose, and in the line of approach. What, then, should decide these differences if not the audience addressed? The answer is simple enough: the questions to be asked and answered. What and how the historian writes depends not on the capacity of those for whom he writes but solely on what he is trying to do about history. Whatever he is there trying to do, he must attempt with a full equipment, a full understanding, a total involvement, and a best use of language, all these qualities being deployed simply to one purpose—to answer his question. Only in this way can he serve the true purpose of history, its contribution to the intellectual improvement of mankind. If instead he decides to entertain, to preach or make propaganda, to persuade people that all is progress or all is disaster, to attract an audience by playing down to them, to follow in fact any purpose other than the sovereign demand of historical study, he not only betrays his calling and his integrity, but he will be found out. When it comes to these matters of high principle it is always well to have some mundane sanctions in hand; and the sort of historian who prides himself simply on selling a lot of his books, or on pleasing an audience, should sometimes listen to what he likes to think are the voices of envy proceeding from less successful colleagues. There is absolutely nothing wrong with selling a lot of books or delighting an audience: solitude guarantees no virtue, nor is there vice in the pleasure of communicating with many. But it is fatal to elevate these considerations above all others. The reactions of one's fellows offer a reasonably true barometer by which to measure one's own sense of standards; and if their criticism were to grow not only contemptuous but justifiably so, the larger multitude, too, will not be long in discovering the truth. Those who barter their soul are especially to be pitied if in the process they lose the world as well.

Thus, the real differences evident in historical writing derive from the differences inherent in what one wants to say. And here, at last, there are hierarchies, or at least there is a line drawn between the higher and the lower. All pursuit of historical truth is, as I have said, respectable, but some forms are less respectable than others. To elucidate this statement it is necessary to classify historical writings by their manner, content and purpose.

5 Categories

Historical works belong to one of three categories: description, analysis, and narrative. Though the first two are in practice rarely divorced, and both are often involved in the third, one may for purposes of classification treat them separately. Description attempts to display a manifestation of the past without giving it the dimension of a change in time; for example, an account of a defunct government department or of a medieval village which simply explains the details of their composition and constitution. Analysis is still fundamentally static but sets the situation or thing described in a wider context of adjoining situations and things, studies interrelations, and attempts to establish causal connections and motives. To take an example: in 1536, the English government created a new office, the Court of Augmentations, to administer new revenues coming to the crown. A descriptive account would explain the structure of the Court, set out its officers and their duties, list its income and expenditure, describe its dissolution. Analysis would add such matters as the place of the Court in the general scheme of government, the reasons for a new court, problems of patronage and influence in the appointment of officers, success or failure in terms of administrative purpose and efficiency, the reasons for its abolition. Narrative tells the story, and it is not material how long the time span may be. Thus both a history of the Court of Augmentations which goes chronologically through the fortunes of the seventeen years of its existence, and a narrative of the sixteenth century in which the Court is mentioned as part of a story of government activity, would rightly be classed as narrative history.

The distinction here is one of purpose and manner, not of quality. Description and analysis are likely to arrange the available material by topics, running repeatedly over the same period of time; narrative uses time as the main backbone of its structure and may have to refer repeatedly to the same point or issue as they reappear in the course of the story. Differences in quality exist but do not provide a useful analytical tool; within the range of historical writing, the good and better, the poor and worse, legitimately share the same categories. However, a real qualitative distinction can be made within these three types, or at any rate in the first and last, for it can be maintained that in analysis there are only varieties of competence. Description and narrative, on the other hand, have two guises, one of them higher than the other. Their lower forms are antiquarianism and chronicle; their higher the meaningful description of the past (into which analysis enters almost invariably) and narrative history properly so called. The distinction between higher and lower forms does not arise from the basic method of proceeding and only in a limited sense from the purpose intended. It arises from the quality of mind brought to the task, the degree to which meaningful questions are asked and penetrating answers given, in short from the intellectual content of the product, a quality really only discernible by its impact on other intellects. Whether a piece of description should be classed as antiquarian or historical, a narrative as chronicle or history, is something that only the reader can tell; but in most cases he has little enough difficulty in making up his mind.

Antiquarianism exists in its own right but also where it has no business to be. It may be recognized by a devotion to detail for its own sake : the antiquarian wants to know, not to understand, and it is of little consequence to him what knowledge he is acquiring. One fact is virtually as good as another, and in the event a kind of galloping inflation takes place until the most tinsel facts are treated as at least as good as gold. The proper home of the antiquarian is parish history, local archaeology, genealogy, lawyer's history of the law—the areas where many facts can be accumulated without straining the reasoning or synthesizing capacity of the student. In its proper place it should not be despised, but it should be seen for what it is. The man who thinks the boundaries of the three-acre field as vital to know-ledge as the frontiers of empires, who rejoices in the find of a Roman coin as though he had discovered the arms of the Venus de Milo, is an antiquarian. His work has value of a kind because the facts he collects can in the proper light contribute to the answering of real questions, that is intellectually challenging questions.

It is when antiquarianism pretends to be history that doubts must arise. Too many supposedly 'real' historians seem to think that their work is done when they have completed the finding-out part of it. Among such his-torians, the taint appears in their attitude to others. They are likely to niggle, to suppose that a striking, novel and imaginative piece of historical writing can be demolished by finding a few errors of detail; they are liable to write reviews full of petty corrections and noting the number of misprints.[14] The antiquarian believes in accuracy. So should we all : inaccuracy and error are faults. But a standard of judgment confined to this one criterion is puny and unintelligent, and a willingness to discard others because they fail in this one particular is ungenerous and unwise. Accuracy is the beginning of the work; to the antiquarian kind of historian it becomes its sole end. The well-trained historian who lacks imagination, enterprise, and the courage to make even mistakes speedily lapses into a kind of antiquarianism which has not even the excuse that its preoccupation with the multiplicity of facts makes no pretence at being anything but a harmless end in itself. A good deal of historical study, and a larger part of the teaching of history, are still troubled by the censorious attentions of this species of antiquarian; and it is no answer that at least he avoids and corrects the more flamboyant, probably more dangerous influence of the pretentious, superficial, effect-hunting historians whom

---

[14] Godfrey Davies, a careful scholar devoid of imagination, tried to resist the new ideas forced upon him by Mr Brian Wormald's *Clarendon* (Cambridge, 1951) in a review so full of petty detail that it quite ignored the real insights of the book attacked (*Eng. Hist. Rev.* lxvii, 1952, 271-5). Even a good historian like A. F. Pollard fell into this trap when, happily without success, he tried to destroy S. B. Chrimes's *English Constitutional Ideas of the Fifteenth Century* (Cambridge, 1936), one of the most important investigations of an obscure period to appear in forty years, however disconcerting some of its details may have been (*History*, xxii, 1937-8, 162-4). On the other hand, the seemingly niggly review is justified when it demonstrates that the large conclusions of some book are baseless because they rest on consistent error of detail; for a good example see J. E. Neale's review of C. H. Garrett, *The Marian Exiles* (Cambridge, 1938) in *Eng. Hist. Rev.* liv, 1939, 501-4.

he conceives it his duty to expose. Two evils do not add up to any kind of good. The way to combat the bogus is to do better that which the bogus do badly, not to deny the validity of the creative mind in the study of history.

Chronicle is the narrative expression of antiquarian fact-collecting, a setting down of events one after the other, without considered discrimination or any discernible purpose except merely to record. By no means all the writings called by that name are chronicles in this precise sense; some men traditionally called chroniclers did apply art—purposive selection and interpretative comment—to a degree which makes them a sort of historians.[15] At its purest, the chronicle is really no more than a list, under each year, of supposedly major events; such, for instance, are the city chronicles of medieval London which give a mingle-mangle of civic officers, public events, natural disasters, deaths and executions, without any application of a considering mind. Even less crude productions bear the hallmark of indiscriminate collection rendered at one single level of expression.

No one, of course, would nowadays dream of writing precisely this sort of stuff. But the chronicle—the largely mindless narrative—is not dead; its modern descendant is the university textbook, provided it is sufficiently textbooky and uninspired. What makes a book of history into a historical textbook is, I suppose, in the first instance, the reason for which it was written : it means to offer an aid to teaching rather than deal with a complex of historical questions. There then results a book which is carefully stuffed with often undifferentiated

---

[15] Cf. e.g. V. H. Galbraith, *Historical Research in Medieval England* (Creighton Lecture : London, 1951).

facts, neatly plotted out in assimilable and usually sub-headed sections of very modest length (so that they can be easily 'assigned' for study), marked by that desire to get everything in which produces in the reader an overwhelming feeling that there is nothing in it, and offering its credentials in unclassified book-lists that are as a rule well out of date. Books of this kind come about because they are written for a particular audience rather than for any reason connected with intellectual enquiry. In addition, they are troubled by a convention of comprehensive coverage which forces them into a steady jog-trot through paddocks marked political, economic, art and literature, and so on. Even good textbooks, like some of the contributions to the *Oxford History of England*, suffer from this diffusion of focus which in the worse examples amounts to the absence of any intellectual centre of gravity. Real narrative history therefore differs from this modern example of chronicle-writing by being composed because the historian wishes to say about history something that is to him important (rather than provide a balanced teaching aid) and because he has in his mind a pattern, a scheme of his bit of the past, which is articulated around a central problem. To this point I shall recur.

These inferior forms of historical writing have been discussed at such length because they are far from rare and can, by the inexperienced, be confused with the higher forms of which they are pale and unintelligent reflections. In looking now at the higher forms, I do not propose to consider whether they are always well-executed or successful; I shall assume that they are, since they are capable of being.

6 Length

We have already noted one set of categories into which real historical writing can be fitted—description/analysis (for at this point it becomes impossible to keep them apart) and narrative. That is a division by method and purpose. Another set of categories applies size and scale: the learned article or essay, the particular monograph of book length, and the sometimes multi-volume comprehensive synthesis and account. The differences in both sets of categories impose special demands on the historian, and since they do not coincide the writer's problem is affected by various combinations from among them. He may write a narrative article or a large synthesis composed of purely analytical parts, though no doubt he is more likely to embark upon an analysis of article length or a large narrative book.

The differences determined by the mere size of the work consist, naturally enough, in the scope of the enterprise—the number and extent of the questions asked. An article cannot deal with as much as can a 500-page book (though some 500-page books turn out on closer inspection to be inflated articles). But because an important corollary is often forgotten, the consequences of this obvious fact are not always observed. Each piece of work, whatever its length, must still have its own proper unity. Though an article may be of the same length as a chapter in a book, it is not by any means the same thing, and the frequent practice of publishing unaltered parts of a doctoral dissertation in learned journals has nothing to recommend it. Every piece of historical writing should be self-contained, should set itself a specific task and discharge it completely; and it is the particular task to be discharged, not the possibilities of publication, which determines the category to which the piece belongs. This also means that length alone does nothing to affect intensity : the short piece which deals with only one or very few questions is not for that reason less governed by the need for depth and completeness than is the long study, nor is length to be achieved by padding and dilution. The nature of the question rules all.

It is, however, true that certain kinds of question demand answers at article length and others call for books. And here a somewhat paradoxical situation arises. The more particular the question and the more restricted the purpose, the shorter will be the answer. So much is obvious. But it is less obvious that the concern with detail, the attention to the evidence, will also be more intensive as the view is narrowed. Thus one valid distinction introduced by differences in length lies in the growing distance from the primary material that increasing size brings with it. An article, to be soundly done, must deal exclusively with the problems set by the historical evidence at its most particular.[16] As the work expands to include more questions and more ranging answers, derived conclusions rather than analysis of the evidence itself increasingly, and rightly, take their place by the side of the use of sources. The historian is perfectly entitled to build not only from the raw material of history but also from the smaller units created out of it by other historians, or by himself in another place, and the larger his view gets the more he will have to do this. One purpose of the learned article, therefore, is to

[16] This applies to creative and original work. Commentary— writing about other people's work, by way of summary or criticism—is a perfectly legitimate activity in itself, but it does not here concern us.

resolve specific and detailed points at issue so that only the answer, not the argument, may be absorbed into a larger whole. This is not to say at all that writing an article is somehow less worthy than writing a book, nor that this contribution to bigger units constitutes the article's sole service in life. Some questions, independent and interesting in themselves, call for no more than twenty or thirty pages to answer them. Description and analysis of a class of evidence, for instance, or the clarification of a judicial or administrative process, belong to this type; their usefulness to others does not involve inclusion in a bigger building but instruction in the use of that building's components. Nor are articles necessarily easier to write than books, though no doubt they take less time to produce and make fewer calls on the historian's ability to construct an argument and hold a great variety of detail and thought in his mind. Too many articles betray an inability to construct by being clearly chopped off at beginning and end. All historical writing must be complete in itself—must argue a case which seems to arise naturally from the evidence and is concluded with the last full stop. Writers of articles need, by and large, to think rather more about what they are trying to do. The institutional demand for published work explains but does not excuse the frequent appearance of dull or somewhat pointless pieces. The man who has nothing to say cannot disguise the fact by putting down his notes in a sort of connected sequence. That, once again, is antiquarianism—history without a mind in it.

These conditions—the restricted range of the point to be made and determined concentration on the real evidence—are likely to mean that a learned article will appeal to fewer readers, or at least will be read by fewer. But this does not absolve the historian from his obligations as an artist. Good writing, clear exposition, wit and life should no more be missing from an article than from a book enshrining a man's life's work. Dullness can never become a virtue, and dullness produced by (as so often it is) mere caution in the face of possible criticism is the proper reward of cowardice. No one wishes to encourage brilliance for mere brilliance' sake, and a sound regard for difficulties expressing itself in well-guarded statements deserves respect. But no one should write until he has achieved a clear view of the answer to his question, and when he has that view he must not allow professional fears to inhibit free expression nor haste to override his concern for lucidity and precision, any more than he must let a childish desire to startle lead him into spurious liveliness. The composition of a short piece, dealing with a real issue, is the best training that the beginner can have in the practice of his craft, but it will serve this purpose only if all the rules of the craft are observed as they would be for a 'real' book—depth of research as well as range of imagination, full exposition as well as living language. Even a technical article should be a pleasure to read and hold interest for the non-specialist.

Still, a technical article is technical and therefore makes demands on knowledge and interest which will restrict its attraction to those who possess a measure of both. As the scope of the work enlarges, as the questions range wider and the issues multiply, that restriction will, or should, progressively disappear. Yet increasing appeal should grow naturally from the subject and its treatment, not be achieved by additions (self-conscious art, unorganic brilliance, stucco decorations) or omissions (avoidance of the difficult, simplification of the complex, concessions to the reader). However large the work and however universal its content, it must still fulfil the demands made of even the smallest good article: it must ultimately and provenly rest on valid interpretations of valid evidence, it must be organized around an intelligent and intelligible argument, and it must be written with clarity and vigour. It should embody a sort of sober pride and sound conviction of professional craftsmanship.

7 *Analysis and Narrative*

This means that once the difference between an article and a book is passed little is to be gained by looking further at mere length. What matters now is the distinction between analysis and narrative, between the dissection of a topic and the telling of a story. An article or essay can, as has been said, be used for either of these tasks, though in the nature of things questions restricted enough to be exhausted in less than thirty pages are likely to call for analysis. Books can do both, and obviously do do both, sometimes inside one set of covers. Which is the method to be preferred? The nature of the question must determine the choice: this needs no labouring. But (as seems sometimes to be held) is one method 'better'—more serious, more distinguished, even more respectable—than the other? And are there rules to be observed or pitfalls to be avoided in either?

It is a fairly common error to suppose that narrative and analysis answer, respectively, the questions 'how' and 'why'. Those questions, together with 'what' and 'when' and 'who', underlie all historical discussion, no matter what form it may take. Nor can analysis overlook the fact of time, or narrative ignore the simultaneous occurence of divers events; otherwise the former would not be history (it might be something like sociology) and the latter would be chronicle. The real question to which analysis in the main addresses itself is 'what was it like', while narrative concentrates on the question 'how did it happen'. The analytical method takes a problem, or a complex of problems, and investigates them by dissecting them into their component parts and their relationships. Narrative, of course, tells the story. The first, therefore, requires a table of topics; it organizes its subject matter under headings and deals with each head in turn. The second arranges things in a series of happenings and divides its matter in the main into chronologically consecutive segments. Both are legitimate methods and both must consider significant questions. However, fashion supposes that analysis is superior; narrative is at present under a cloud. The historian who tells a story is supposed to be a little undemanding at best, superficial and ignorant at worst. To study problems not periods was Lord Acton's much-quoted injunction, and those who cite him approvingly fail to note that it is now some seventy years since he uttered those gnomic words, and that in actual fact he proved incapable of studying either problems or periods to a practical conclusion. The historian, working in the records and meeting one unresolved problem after another, quite naturally persuades himself that the real work consists in tackling these dark entities, and nearly always it is perfectly true that they will yield only to the analytical method. But that does not mean that one should pin a special medal on analysis. Since history is the record of events, and of problems, proceeding through time, narrative must be not only legitimate but also urgently called for.

Once again, the only point which determines the choice is the historian's purpose, the questions he is asking. The complete historian must ask both what it was like and how it happened, and he can ask this either at different times (that is, in different books) or occasionally at one and the same time; he must not think of the method of ordering his thoughts as something imposed on him from outside, by training or convention; and he must cultivate both techniques in equal measure. Thus he must thoroughly acquaint himself not so much with the peculiar characteristics of each—these are not obscure—as with the dangers and difficulties which beset them.

The main danger inherent in the analytical method is that it fragments the unity of the historical process. I am not here thinking of Professor Hexter's 'tunnel history', the use of categories like political, economic or intellectual history to circumscribe the work done.[17] Nobody can write universal history—everything that happened or has been thought—in one piece; the processes of writing will not permit it. These 'tunnels' are necessary mechanisms, and history so divided up can in each case yield to both the analytical and the narrative approach. The point is that, within the necessarily circumscribed section of history which the historian can manage, analysis still runs the danger of fragmentation.

Up to a point, this is inescapable. Topics do not occur in isolation, but if they are to be discussed in turn they are liable to give that impression. The first rule to be observed is that an analytically organized book must still be a book, not a series of articles. There must be a common theme to hold the topics together, and chapters must appear to run on naturally one from another. The order in which these more or less parallel topics are introduced is vitally important: it should have a discernible logic in it. Every device, however

[17] See above, p. 28.

superfluous it may seem, should be employed to underline coherence and continuity. Each new topic should be linked to its predecessor by lead-over and pick-up sentences, and the general question of the book should be kept constantly in mind and frequently before the reader. Thus, suppose one were to write a book on the Industrial Revolution in England (a not uncommon thing to do). This is a theme which cries out for the analytical treatment, as all the various elements in the story (agricultural reform, technological advance, changes in population and labour force, capital market and rate of interest, and so on) pass before the historian's mind. No one could possibly assemble them into a useful single narrative. But a mere series of chapters on these topics would be neither a good book nor a real exposition and explanation of the phenomenon studied. If the task is to be properly discharged, each element, as it is analysed in turn, must contribute directly to an understanding of a major movement which must at the same time become comprehensible in its passage through time. This suggests that the historian should isolate for himself a main thread in a story he does not propose to tell as a story. He may choose what thread he pleases—for instance, increase of production, or the role of the entrepreneur. Having chosen it, he cannot profitably abandon it : he will have to write each section not as a self-contained account of that part of the panorama he happens to be dealing with, but deliberately as part of an account of his main theme. Swapping horses in mid-book destroys books. The analytical historian is composing not a mosaic but a painting in which the canvas is covered several times over with different pigments and patterns, until an amalgam of colour and design emerges from the repeated process. This metaphor has its dangers because it does not permit the introduction of a movement through time which should also be apparent from the book, but it will give a hint of the right idea.[18]

Analysis can be very static and prevent an understanding of change: this is one major danger to guard against. In the example I chose, of the Industrial Revolution, the danger is not great because each element in the story clearly calls for some progressive treatment. But analytical books, even good ones, often fall into this trap which is sprung by failure to realize that evidence taken from a given period of time must be evaluated against the background of change involved in temporal progress. To use, for instance, evidence from the beginning and end of a long period as though it necessarily belonged to one and the same order of fact is to run into trouble. How seriously this can affect the best work is demonstrated by Christopher Hill's fine book on *The Economic Problems of the Church from Archbishop Whitgift to the Long Parliament* (Oxford, 1956). Its arrangement is entirely analytical: four topic-chapters on 'The State of the Clergy', six on the financial problems, four on the work of Archbishop Laud. No other arrangement could have brought out so well the condition of Church and clergy or the situation faced by them, and no other could have provided such thorough discussion of problems like tithe or

[18] Two recent books illustrate the point. T. S. Ashton's concise study of *The Industrial Revolution* (London, 1948) is held together by the author's conviction that the clue to the story is found in the fluctuations of the rate of interest. Though he was probably wrong in this, he was able to write a well-articulated book. On the other hand, Phyllis Deane's *The First Industrial Revolution* (Cambridge, 1965) is really a collection of separate essays on various aspects, held together by no single line of argument; and it reads like that. The work grew out of a course of lectures, always a difficult thing to turn into a real book.

pluralism. But a treatment which collects its facts indiscriminately from a period of sixty years, as though in that time such things as Puritanism or the complaints against the hierarchy had not passed through profoundly changing attitudes, purposes and ambitions, creates a very misleading air of sameness by the simple device of assuming that nothing changed. The analysis itself is distorted because the transformations of the historical situation are ignored; people's thoughts and actions are seen in unreal isolation from changing circumstances. This is by no means an indictment of the analytical method (though it forms a legitimate, if limited, criticism of this book), but it constitutes a warning to remember the story when dissecting components. To be satisfactory, analysis must incorporate narrative. That is to say, while the fundamental organization of any book asking 'what was it like' should be by topics and sections, each topic must not only be organically linked to the rest but must also run through time and remember change.

However, if the question obviously posed by the purpose of a book is 'what happened', then analysis must not be allowed to usurp the place of narrative. It is here that the present dislike of story-telling as a historical method introduces real perils. The historian faced with the task of writing an account of some large piece of history—the history of a country, a continent, or an age—cannot avoid a basic structure which concentrates on the chronological, even chronicle, element, the passage through the years. Otherwise he cannot possibly convey the essential feel of time passing, men succeeding each other, lives being lived and deaths being died. He may well come to the conclusion that of some topics he has to treat separately; he may require analytical chapters, though whether he should surrender to this supposed need is something to be discussed in a moment. But he cannot allow himself a mainly analytical structure. To take, once again, by way of example, a book good enough to stand such critical regard : Christopher Brooke's *Europe in the Central Middle Ages* (London, 1964). This is one volume in a general cooperative history of Europe and covers the years 962 to 1154. Nearly two hundred years, a time of much change; and Europe is a sufficiently large area. There can be no question of a single main problem being here dissected into its parts. Yet of Professor Brooke's eighteen chapters, no fewer than ten are strictly analytical and the rest, embodying sections of narrative, follow in the main an analytical approach. The difficulties of narrating the confused and multiple history of those years are indeed formidable; yet it is hard to be satisfied with a treatment which by some 100 pages separates chapters on certain emperors and certain popes whose lives were spent in conflict with each other. The result is that the book lacks a main thread. Quite possibly the feeling that things happen higgledy-piggledy, here, there and everywhere, reflects a reality; it could well represent the feelings of such contemporaries as were alert enough to think of their world at all. But the historian's task is to explain—to make plain—and in order to do so he has to discover and elaborate his theme. I am not expert enough on that age to suggest one with confidence, but one can imagine a book working out the emergence of a particular civilization, dominated by a reformed and aggressive Church on the one hand and locally ascendant monarchies on the other, which would firmly organize its narrative of kings, popes, emperors and thinkers to that end.

To say this, however, is at once to call up the retort that to write a narrative of emperors and popes is to do very little justice to the realities of history. The current preference for what is called social history demands a progressive analysis and account of societies (politically and socially identifiable groups of people) at all their levels and in their multifarious appearances, not only as agents of political action but also as producers of wealth, harbourers of internal conflict, promoters of intellectual enterprise; and it is not perhaps much of an answer that hardly any such books in fact exist. How can narrative possibly manage to render the complexities of such a story, and is it not therefore inevitably condemned to superficiality, for ever recalling the simple chronicle from which it grew? While history confined itself to the doings of governments, so runs the argument, narrative was a proper and satisfactory method, but we have left all that behind. The long ascendancy of Ranke, primarily concerned with international relations and diplomacy, themes thoroughly amenable to the narrative method, has been replaced by such influences as that of the French *Annales* school which wishes to understand a whole society in every detail, in all its interrelations and activities, and therefore insists on analysis. Compare a work like Prescott's *History of the Reign of Philip II* with Fernand Braudel's *La Méditerranée et le monde méditerranéen à l'époque de Philippe II* (Paris, 1949), and the change becomes very apparent. The second book offers some splendid understanding of the circumstances which contributed to the shaping of policy and action; the only things missing are policy and action. There is a clear and admirable sense of life, but how those lives passed through history is much less clear. To me, at least, the *Annales* method—certainly until it lost itself in rhetoric and self-adulation—represents a valuable, perhaps necessary, stage in the development of historical writing, one which attacked genuine deficiencies and did a good deal to remedy them, but it must not be regarded as in some way the sole consummation of the historian's duties. In many fields of history it is either clearly insufficient or has already done its work. Legitimate in itself, and in such hands as Bloch's or Braudel's remarkably successful, it can no more answer all the important questions of history than can any other method.

Unhappily, any attempt to restore narrative to a respectable place in the historian's armoury runs into the reformer's most awkward problem: the friends he makes and the unwanted allies that surround him. It cannot be denied that a good deal of the occasional clamour against 'technical' and analytical history, or the sort of praise for story-telling one encounters in the worthier lay periodicals, arises from intellectual indolence and a desire for popular success. It is perfectly possible to feel respect and liking for the writings of the serious popular historians without believing that theirs is the highest form of history or the model to follow. Among them are notable practitioners of a far from easy skill; it would not be difficult to bias the argument by looking at the lesser lights; but even the best lack the searching depth of investigation, the establishment of solid truths, and the accumulation of fruitfully illuminating explanations which professional history must and can provide. However hard it may be to write flowing narrative or to evoke people and places, it should not be doubted that the intellectual effort involved in real analysis and its presentation is markedly greater. In addition, much narrative history helps itself by ignoring unsolved questions, accepting ready-made explanations, repeating stale argument at second hand; and narrative that depends on art superficially imposed on simplicity or ignorance does indeed merit the strictures of the austerer scholars. The question is whether other forms of narrative are possible, and I think they are.

The defender of historical narrative as a profound form of writing history faces one further handicap in the prevalence of biographies. Though biography is really a separate art, with rules and problems of its own, most people seem to think of it as simply a form of history; yet, in so far as it is history, it tends to underline the potential weakness of narrative. It is certainly historical, and it is bound to be narrative in its main structure. Since it deals with an individual's life it possesses a given beginning and a known end between which the sequence of events runs clearly in one direction. The biographer thus has his first problem solved for him : neither the limits of his study nor its basic structure are open to choice. Now in England, at least, biographies are innumerable; their production forms one of the country's most flourishing industries, and they are well liked by readers. Whatever may be true of the bulk of them, quite a few are admirable. What matters here is that even at its best biography is a poor way of writing history. The biographer's task is to tell the story, demonstrate the personality, and elucidate the importance of one individual; he should not be concerned with the history of that individual's times except in so far as it centres upon or emanates from him. In measure as he deserts his proper subject for what concerns the historian, that subject's age, he fails in his own task. Very occasionally, a 'great man's' life may prove a tool useful for opening a problem of history—some kings or statesmen can serve this purpose—but even when the tool is useful it is not the best available. The limits of one man's life rarely have any meaning in the interpretation of history; even if his death marks a period (and how rarely this happens) his birth will not. However influential he may have been, no individual has ever dominated his age to the point where it becomes sensible to write its history purely around him. And, above all, those parts of his career that may carry the greatest historical significance are not likely to be those on which a biographer should mainly concentrate. He should give much weight to those private relationships and petty concerns which have little to tell the historian; in particular, if he is to understand his subject's personality, he should deal thoroughly with those formative years during which the history of the age is likely to be quite unaware of the growing man. None of this speaks against biography as a form of writing, but it does mean that biography is not a good way of writing history. The historian should know the histories and characters of many men, as he should know much else, but he should not write biography—or at least should not suppose that in writing biography he is writing history. The low esteem in which biography is often held—not without reason—therefore offers no argument at all against narrative history : the two are different things.

What, then, should narrative do to avoid the charges of superficiality, intellectual weakness, inability to deal with the real questions—charges that are often raised against it by professional historians? If a narrative form could be found which would enable the historian to offer real explanations of problems and to accommodate more than the traditional political story, the genre would again become respectable, especially if at the same time it could preserve its special distinction as literary art. In this endeavour, the narrative historian confronts two technical problems : the definition of a theme, and the discovery of a structure which amalgamates with this theme historical points and problems not directly arising from it.

In defining his theme, the historian must first of all establish meaningful limits, points in time which give to his narrative a true sense of coherence. Any old bit cut out of the interminable flow of time will still be history, but it will not be good history because it will lack purpose and so will not enable the writer to create a work of thought and art. In practice, the limits may well be provided by the main theme chosen. The narrative historian necessarily decides to tell the story of something—of a nation, a political organization, a Church, a government, a business, or whatever may come to mind among the activities of men, or of some phase in that story which interests him. When he has chosen his theme, its limits should come to him as a matter of course, but it is still worth saying that he should from first to last be aware of the need to have real limits and should so construct his story that it naturally runs from one to the other. Few themes do in fact run from one clearly defined point in time to another, but this does not permit the writer to delay the opening of his narrative with long scene-setting chapters or to drag it out into lengthy perspectives and forecasts at the end. If scenes are to be set and consequences be made plain, this should be done inside the narrative; narrative history at its most effective demands that no clearly defined sections be blatantly analytical.

The kind of theme chosen may also pose serious problems. If the history is to deal with a restricted body of men, things may be easy. A history of the East India Company or Imperial Chemical Industries, of the king's Chancery or the Methodist Church, will naturally be written along a main line defined by the fortunes of those organizations. But narrative history often has to deal with groups of men expressing themselves in different ways or living side by side in entanglement and separateness, as it might be a nation which has a political, social, economic, religious and intellectual history; or it deals with an age in which a number of such societies can all claim to have lived such varied lives. Here the historian must choose a main theme, often a very hard choice but not one to be avoided by running a number of themes alongside each other in separate chapters. The historian may suppose that his choice depends on his own preference, and to some extent this enters into it. But there are two chief considerations that really determine the main theme : the availability of evidence, and the need to find a theme sufficiently dominant to carry the others along with it.

In practice, it has to be admitted, this means that the main theme even to-day will be nearly always 'political' : it must consist of the actions of governments and governed in the public life of the time. For all ages before about 1800 the vast bulk of the surviving evidence bears on such topics, and even thereafter that kind of evidence predominates. And secondly, since narrative is necessarily a record of events succeeding each other, it is necessarily the record of action (and suffering); and the most manifest, continuous and purposeful action is that which guides a community through its life and its relations with other communities. Thus political narrative—the doings of the rulers and the reactions of the ruled at all levels—still stands out as the probable main thread of any narrative. The history of Tudor England can be written as the history of sheep-farming, or of vernacular poetry, or of maritime enterprise, or of doctrinal debate; other themes could be found. But none of these lines runs clean down the middle because they do not involve a large enough part of the people living at the time nor a large enough part of the evidence. None of them make it easy to accommodate the others in the same story. As main themes they are therefore inferior to politics—the activities of government—for which the evidence is thickest and to which other themes most readily relate.

However, it is perfectly true that mere political history is not enough. A plain tale of wars and treaties, elections and reforms, the fortunes of the great, however well it may be told, can no longer satisfy our conception of history or accommodate our knowledge of it. In order that action may be understood, its setting, circumstances and springs must be made plain, and these are found not only in the psychology of individuals and crowds, but especially in the details of administration, the economy, the intellectual preoccupations of the time, and all other so-called 'factors'. The narrative historian comes up against separate problems that either have been solved and must be absorbed, or that have to be solved by him, before he can continue his story. It is his task to accommodate such matters, which require analytical treatment, in such a way that the narrative seems hardly to be interrupted at all. This means that he should not treat of them as plainly separate entities, in separate chapters or sections clearly marked off. Rather they should be erratic boulders carried along in the glacier flow—paragraphs, sometimes sentences, which seem to come naturally at some point of the narrative and slip readily into its continuation, so that the reader is barely aware of the change of pace. (In itself, a change of pace is desirable in any prolonged account.) To be satisfactory, and in order to avoid the charge of superficiality, historical narrative must, as it were, be thickened by the results of analysis. This requires the historian to gather together every aspect and every turn of the subject matter, digest it comprehensively in the mind, and use it to elaborate the points of his narrative.

While it would help to illustrate these probably obscure

prescriptions, I feel unable to do so without displaying the conceit involved in citing my own example. This kind of narrative is what I attempted in my *Reformation Europe* (London, 1963). The book avoids the customary scene-setting at the start. Instead it goes straight into the story of Luther's rebellion, whch naturally calls for some description of the man; this introduces, as a matter of course, the points of theology over which he rebelled. Once the narrative is well under way, it demands some understanding of Luther's success in the circumstances of time and place, which necessitates a long—possibly by these rules too long—discussion of 'the state of Germany'. Because this comes after the narrative has begun, and not by way of introducing Luther's action, it seems to me to avoid the appearance of a separate and unintegrated chapter, though in this I may, of course, be quite mistaken. Smaller problems are more easily accommodated. The account of Charles V's wars with the French can be arrested for a couple of paragraphs to analyse the military practice of the time; his involvement with the Turks can be used to slip in a description of that despotism. And so on. It is perfectly true that those aspects of the age which yield best to thoroughly analytical treatment will not come across in such detail as another approach might provide; the point is that I was trying to write the kind of narrative in which analytical chunks are somehow embedded without destroying the sense of action, movement, time passing, across the whole range of problems. Certainly I did not succeed completely : if I had, I should have been able to do without a chapter on 'The Age'—parts of which, it now seems to me, could have been treated in the course of the narrative. There are some other passages where analysis seems to me to threaten the narrative, or at least to hold it suspended for rather too long. I cite this example only because I did try to practise what here I preach, and I think I had some measure of success with it; I managed to discuss topics and argue points not usually encountered in books treating narratively and concisely of controversial and intellectually complex periods. The method is possible, but it still needs a great deal of thought and work to improve it.

In actual fact, it need not be doubted that the ideally pure form of this sort of narrative can never be written. The complexities of every story are too great, and the historian must lose his worth if either through ignorance or by design he solves his problem by leaving out the awkward things. To some, a traditional method, alternating narrative and analytical chapters, may seem preferable, because it is more easily done and less likely to omit matters, but I do not like it so well. I am, however, inclined to think that large-scale history cannot be written without *some* patently analytical sections which I regard as inescapable setbacks in a battle that must on balance be won. If the question is 'what happened', the answer must tell a story, and however 'thickened' or interrupted that story turns out to be it must continuously keep the reader moving through the years. People must palpably be born, grow up and die; institutions, organizations, societies must be seen to change and vary; events must clearly follow one upon another. Everything must most manifestly be taking place in time. And yet the deeper insight into problems, the discussions of unsettled or doubtful points, the hard intellectual digging which analysis alone can provide must also be ever present as the tale proceeds: not only present to the historian, but by him also communicated, integrated in the flow of time, to all who read.

Narrative of this sort, however short of the ideal, is

not, of course, easy to write. It challenges the constructive skills of the writer as well as his ability to hold together a great number of traces that keep pulling apart. It is much harder to do than analytical history which, in turn, may well require more concentrated and intensive thought. Neither is, however, superior to the other, and he who dissects problems need not look down upon the narrator as a mere teller of tales, nor need the story-teller despise the concerns of his analysing colleague as absence of imagination. The complete historian, in any case, is both. Both are truly important forms of intelligent and intellectual activity, proper to be reckoned among the more respected occupations of the human mind. Within the single task of understanding and recreating the past, they serve different and complementary purposes. Still, I confess to a personal hankering after the sort of narrative I have described. I find it more difficult to accomplish than the analysis of historical problems, and therefore more exciting to do. It needs even more art, more transformation of the raw material. But personal preferences should not be mistaken for general rules, even by him who holds them.

It should be plain by now that though I believe in the independence of history and the possibility of discovering a right truth by the techniques of scholarship, I do not hold that these facts result in historical writing independent of the writer. Quite often this dependence does not interfere with the statement of manifest and incontrovertible truth; there are a good many problems in history, large and small, for which nobody now manages to work up any bias or prejudice. At other times it does interfere. Add the uncertainties of historical writing—the gaps in the evidence, the frequent obscurity of what does survive, the need to read and interpret with a controlled imagination, the demands of order and sense—and it is plain enough that no work is free of the tentative, the doubtful, the correctable. Yet what of that? Why should this limit the historian's desire to know and to write, or his claim to be listened to? Only those to whom the insufficiencies of the human existence are anathema could ever suppose that it should, and people of that cast of mind have no cause to concern themselves with men or their history.

The historian fulfils his function properly if, aware of the unsolved and insoluble problems, conscious that he is not a machine and can be moved by love, anger, contempt and vanity, he concentrates on honesty and integrity. He must become a scholar, which is to say that he must add a dimension to his humanity, not remove one. And he will be wise to cultivate the sceptic mind, a reserved and questioning attitude to all claimed certainties, for as long as he can. He needs to be learned, balanced, imaginative, able to see all points of view and yet to assess them from one of his own. Imagination will give life to his learning, learning will direct the sweep of his imagination. Over all should rule a searching intelligence, asking that fundamental question of the sceptic : just what do you mean by that? And if that question is asked with a real desire to know and understand, if the imagination is centred upon people—dead people once alive—and sympathy and judgment are controlled by scholarship and by a mind of quality, the work can be done. All the deficiencies of knowledge and writer notwithstanding, the historian can rest assured that he can fulfil his ambition to know and tell about the past. His can never be the last word, an ambition in any case bred out of vanity, but he can establish new footholds in the territory of truth.

IV

Teaching

The vast majority of professional historians nowadays earn their living as teachers. Though there remain a few whom private means or successful books enable to dispense with employment, and though historians can be found on the staffs of archives, libraries and museums, the typical member of the profession divides his time between his researches and the instruction of the young. The whole training scheme, built round the much abused Ph.D., is designed to produce teachers who use the mould they have stepped from to fashion more men (and women) in their own image. The expansion of university education all over the world has in the last twenty years altered the proportions in which these men divide their time: teaching takes up more of it than once it did, and those professors who use their eminence and effrontery to redress the balance in their own lives only succeed by placing more of the burden on others. For that it can be a burden is true enough and need not be denied; anything is that interferes with lotus-eating. Everybody at all acquainted with these matters has heard the frequent laments about the way in which teaching interferes with a man's 'own work', and nobody, however dedicated a teacher he may be, can have passed through even a few years of his career without feeling at times that these complaints are justified.

It is therefore worth stressing—as the great mass of

competent and conscientious university teachers know perfectly well—that the two sides of the work are equally necessary and mutually complementary. Teaching not only enables a man to eat and therefore live in the pursuit of the truth; it also makes him a better historian. And the teacher who has ceased to take part in the work of exploration, discovery and restatement is very unlikely to remain a useful instructor. Only continuous first-hand experience of the way in which history should be studied and written maintains the ability to convey it to others with a sense of purpose and inspiration. This would probably be readily agreed to by most, and recognition of the fact justifies, to some extent, the demands for 'production' which university administrators so often make on their professors. (Not that they demand it for this reason : though blind, they may sometimes tread well.) What is less widely realized is the truth of the reverse : that the constant experience of teaching is at least a very important preserver of scholarly energies and standards. It would be possible to adduce examples to show how able historians have deteriorated as they have abandoned teaching. The man who has to explain himself to others and to excite their excitement, and who has to do this in inescapable conditions of personal contact, finds that he is thereby controlling and improving his performance as an historian no less than as a teacher. I remember many occasions on which attempts to explain something to a student suddenly brought into focus the components of a problem, for the first time showed me where accepted interpretations had been too easily accepted, or by making me think afresh made me reorganize a mass of material of which the student, the stimulus to it all, could not even be aware. Teaching of necessity creates its own form of arrogance; the position of preceptor, the claims of seniority, contain strong elements of assured superiority, and instruction must at times be didactic. But teaching also provides an opportunity for humility and a discipline in precise thought and even more precise expression, and the historian who never has to try his knowledge and ideas on an audience physically present and able to interrogate him misses one of his most useful experiences.

Thus the double existence of scholar and teacher is not only an economic and sociological necessity but a convenient and profitable thing for the working historian. This means that he would do well to give some thought to what he is doing not only as an historian but also as a teacher. The necessary association of his two activities, research and instruction, in fact itself reflects the fundamental difficulty involved in teaching, a difficulty much greater in history than in some more precise subjects. Can history be taught at all? Teaching is conventionally supposed to be a process of instruction, whether by the simple transfer of knowledge from one mind to another or by the evocation in the mind taught of the learning and understanding present in the mind teaching. Yet history is a subject in which the learned dispute as much as they agree; progress in it comes as often through an argumentative study of old problems as through the solving of new ones. Certainly there is an agreed body of knowledge to be transmitted, but no one supposes that such transmission constitutes the teaching of history. On the one hand, it is much too big a task : in the few years that a man can set aside in his life for his student days, no one can 'teach' him all that is firmly known in history. On the other hand, it is perfectly obvious that instruction which confines itself to expounding some knowledge and demanding its absorption by the student does not deserve the name of teaching because nothing of value is done to the student mind. The study of history consists of debates— between the historian and his evidence, between different students of history, between the historian and his own society—and if the teaching of history is to be successful it, too, must rest on debate. All teaching requires the active participation of both the teacher and the taught; in history, this is made more necessary as well as more difficult by the fact that the mere conveying of knowledge runs up against both the enormous and unorganizable quantity of that knowledge and the debatable uncertainties which alone give meaning to that knowledge.

In this discussion it will therefore be taken for granted that, though all teaching involves some straight infusion of facts and figures, history cannot be taught in the sense that any student can, by teaching, be made to possess a sufficient, coherent, self-satisfactory body of knowledge. No doubt this is true of all fields of study, but in the natural sciences, for instance, or in engineering and medicine, teaching must aim at instilling a grasp of agreed knowledge which, as it is added to by research, also sheds points proved erroneous and thus continues to be a teachable entity, namely the subject in question. Just enough of this happens in history, where also elements once thought true can be removed by the process of research, to justify a large measure of normal teaching activity; but here one important consequence of new knowledge is to put old knowledge into new light, not to destroy it, so that what might at one time be a manageable entity soon becomes too large, too subtle, and too diffuse to be taught in this sense. A subject in which no one can rewrite the standard textbook—in which, indeed, there can be no standard textbook, no Gray's *Anatomy* regularly renewed through the generations—obviously poses problems of a very different order.

If 'history', not being a subject like anatomy or molecular chemistry, cannot itself be taught, the purpose of teaching history must be different from that of teaching medicine or law; the end in view cannot be simply assumed but needs thought. In the main, that end differs with the class of persons taught. I shall not concern myself with the teaching of schoolchildren, though I have practised it (rather badly) in my time. Perhaps because I have tried to do it, I have developed serious doubts about the wisdom of doing it at all. History deals with the activities of men, not of abstractions, and a measure of maturity is really necessary before the student can understand what is before him and is being said to him. The intellect may well be at its brightest before experience comes to tarnish it and confuse every issue : chess players and mathematicians do well to register their achievements young. But in history only experience and insight can save the intellect from its characteristic fault of over-simplifying and over-organizing every problem, and even at eighteen, when mankind is most certain that it knows everything, it is easy to mistake absence of understanding for clarity of vision. In a very real sense, history is not a good subject to teach to children, or rather, the 'real' thing—academic history—is the wrong thing for them. What may be right shall not be enquired into here. I must confine myself to the academic teaching of academic history, which means that I shall consider the problems of teaching history at a university. These naturally divide into the teaching of undergraduate and graduate students, not only because the two groups differ in age, attainment and the particular knowledge they seek, but more fundamentally because the purposes of teaching them are quite different.

1 Undergraduate Teaching: What?[1]

In the history departments of British universities, at least, 'syllabus reform' is a game played in an atmosphere heavy with suspicion and ambition; the rolled logs, clattering by, at times drown the very voice of the teacher, and instead of pursuing 'their own work' scholars draft memoranda to one another. The more enterprising and less scrupulous publish their pet schemes in the press and on the air, gaining a reputation for advanced thought and an exclusive hearing for one side. The motives behind the turmoil vary a good deal. There is fear: history is losing students to such other disciplines as English or the social sciences and must be made more attractive. (This fear is sometimes voiced by those who complain most loudly of the burden imposed on them by excessive student numbers.) There is self-interest: the man who has specialized in something not prominent in the syllabus understandably enough wants to change that sad state of affairs. There is resentment: to judge by the feelings entertained by many professional historians, especially of advancing years, for medieval studies, medievalists must in an earlier generation have been most unwisely arrogant.

[1] Nearly all my experience has been with English undergraduates with their high level of specialization at school. This naturally colours what follows, but I believe that the principles which I shall try to distinguish have a wider application, and that the practice which I shall describe can be readily adapted to students who have passed through a different pre-university career. Though there are special difficulties in teaching mass audiences or those for whom history is only part of their course, I think that at heart the problems remain the same and that the answers, while they may vary a little, do not change in essence.

But the main body of the clamour arises from genuine doubts about the value of existing methods and subjects: those who would wish to widen studies by the inclusion of various parts of the world hitherto obscure, or who favour 'interdisciplinary' courses combining history, geography, philosophy, literature, and so forth, are often imaginative and enterprising as well as sincere. Whether they are also wise is another question. New universities, with at first small departments and few students, offer opportunities for experiment, and though not all the experiments have avoided the taint of gimmickry many sound interesting and some are striking.[2] Still, sincerity can be an overrated quality and is assuredly no guarantee of sense. The value of all these experiments and the justice of all these complaints must depend on a more rigorous analysis of the purposes pursued than one commonly encounters. Just what are we trying, just what should we be trying, to do when we teach history to undergraduates?

I have already said that in my view we neither can nor should try to convey a knowledge of history in the sense of simply acquainting the student with a given body of facts or interpretations. We need to do a certain measure of this because our courses must have content, but we cannot restrict our purposes to so low-grade an exercise. If we really had nothing better to do than present a history of England or China, of political thought or economic practice, and afterwards to elicit that same information again by means of examinations, we might as well resign our students to more intelligent disciplines. Yet the frequent demand that insularity

[2] At the newly founded University of Warwick, history students are to spend one term away from base, in either Italy or the United States. This is not only nice for them but nice for their relieved teachers, too.

be replaced by global concerns (or some such phrase)—
that the student should know about Russia or know the
facts of African history—seems to suppose that the
purpose of teaching history is just instruction in information hitherto unknown. A subtler argument starts
from the axiom—which happens to be true—that the
purpose of all university education is to equip men and
women for their lives in the world, and then draws the
conclusion that the contents of the course must therefore change as the place of a man's country changes in
the hierarchy and importance of societies. Thus to
Professor Southern, the predominance of English constitutional history, which has long characterized the
Oxford school, was justified while Great Britain was top
dog and Oxford graduates in history might commonly
expect to employ themselves variously in the government
of an empire. That condition has vanished : therefore,
constitutional history should be replaced by a study of
what alone now gives Englishmen influence, namely
culture and ideas.[8] Does one have to be a crude
imperialist to question the logic of this reasoning? More
straightforwardly, the many who argue that the study of
history should teach the young student to understand
his own time hold that the syllabus needs to be restricted
to recent history, or that it should include compulsory
study of the history of science. It should be said, with
regret, that there is no proof that a knowledge of history,
recent or distant, at B.A. level succeeds in giving a man
much understanding of his own time.

What, to me, seems wrong with all these pleas is that

[8] R. W. Southern, *The Shapes and Substance of Academic
History* (Oxford, 1961). I do not think I misrepresent the argument
of this inaugural lecture which seems to me an unacceptable
plea for the superiority of the study of the mind over the study of
matter.

they look for entirely external conditions to which their programmes must answer. I cannot accept that the study of history should be justified only by such incidental consequences as additions to a man's memorized knowledge or an understanding of this or that situation. As was said earlier on, anyone concerning himself with historical studies in any form should seek their purpose in the intellectual training they provide and in the augmentation they offer to the life of the mind. That greater proposition surely includes this lesser: if the historian may justify his existence by reference to the contribution he makes to the human intellect, the teacher must similarly consider that the purpose of his teaching is to turn out men with improved intellects at their disposal. Three or four years spent at a university cannot teach a man to know history; they cannot train him as a politician or publicist or publisher; they can at best begin to lay some foundations for a view of the world and (universities being what they are) are likely to lay foundations which, as later experience shows, need to be broken up. None of this invites blame: the impossible need not be attempted. But if those years do not produce an effective conditioning of the reasoning mind, if they do not teach a man to think better than otherwise he would have done, they may justly be condemned as a waste of time.

It follows that the purpose of teaching history to undergraduates is to equip them with the special intellectual training embodied in the study of history at any level. This intellectual training consists of two elements: a sharpening of the critical analytical faculty, and a deepening of the imaginative and constructive faculty. Since these are the qualities required in the successful study of history, they are the qualities which the teaching of history is most competent to instil. The study of history involves the analysis of problems in an extensive setting, both temporal and spatial; the student needs to be capable of close reasoning and the sceptical assessment of evidence, but must perform this common scientific duty in such a manner that the surrounding circumstances of his problem, antecedents and consequences, concomitants and contrasts, affect the solution of the specific details of the problem itself. That is what one means by an understanding of history, and it seems only reasonable to suppose that the undergraduate reading history should be instructed in just this kind of understanding. Inasmuch as these abilities are essential to the professional historian, it might be argued that all academic teaching of history concerns itself with the training of professional historians; and I myself believe that in approaching the student one should indeed treat him as a potential scholar of one's own kind. Of course, few of them will in fact choose that career, but that is not the point. The point is, firstly, that the professional scholar teaching others will do best if he stays within his professional competence; he may by all means try to enlighten his pupils about humanity at large, but he will be really successful only if he employs the techniques of his own craft in the elucidation of the subject matter of his teaching. Secondly, it need not be doubted that the special intellectual qualities developed in the scholar and for the potential scholar have a much wider usefulness: no man is the worse for having acquired an ability to analyse problems and to grasp larger wholes imaginatively. Where he applies this ability is of no importance; what does matter is that he should have it, that it rather than the acquiring of a body of knowledge is the proper end of education, and that the study of history is exceptionally well qualified to teach it.

A teaching syllabus must, therefore, be so constructed as to give an opportunity to develop these qualities of the mind. Since all history, properly deployed, can do this, it matters in essence very little what particular sections of it are taught. A course of study should concern itself less with the question whether this or that bit of historical knowledge will be 'useful' to the student than with the more difficult problem of finding topics which, on the one hand, teach the analysis of problems and, on the other, encourage imaginative vision, provoke comparisons, and range through time.

In practice, this means selecting two types of subject. There should be both the particular and the general, the narrow and the wide. Both kinds have their obvious dangers. The particular and narrow can lead to pedantry and immersion in the minute; the wide and general can result in the parroting of superficial, second-hand opinions. Teaching both kinds side by side is probably the best insurance against the dangers inherent in either. All undergraduate courses therefore need to include the study of some large area over a considerable stretch of time, as for instance European history from the first days of the Renaissance to the Enlightenment, or the history of the United States (still short enough to resist subdivision for this purpose). But though the subject may be large, it should still have a coherence of its own; any old lump carved from the body of history will not do. Since the purpose is to train a man in the taking of comprehensive views and the understanding of massive interactions, the subject of his study needs to convey a sense of meaning and singularity. Thus those familiar topics, medieval and modern European history, dividing conventionally round about 1450, are ill-designed for the task, whereas the student who is asked to study the manner in which European intellectual development, reflected in politics and economics as well, took up the influence of Renaissance thought and practice and worked it out until the temporary eighteenth-century synthesis emerged, is faced with a specific defined problem which happens to be large in extent and implications, and instructive in the way in which it compels the student to follow lines in all directions while holding a meaningful interpretation in the mind. A large and general subject should not be diffuse; rigour of a kind, provided by the fact of coherence, must still be sought.

Admittedly, some good judges hold that, since history is a whole which, for purely practical purposes, has unfortunately to be cut up, the knife should be inserted at some totally meaningless point, some date of no significance. In this way, so runs the argument, the student is saved both from the prearranged meaning given to an historical problem by his teacher and from the false supposition that terminal dates are fundamental realities. If the dates of his subject manifestly begin and end nothing, he will the more readily remember that the problem he studies reaches back and continues further than he has time to take it, so that he will get a more positive grasp of the continuous flow of history through time. Also, he will be able to see things in a fresh light, whereas meaningful terminal dates themselves condition the answer to be discovered. There is a good deal in this argument, and my only reason for preferring the possibly more old-fashioned construction of a teaching subject coherent in itself is that in practice it is likely to work better. To the trained historian, the moving, or removal, of conventional landmarks is one of the most fruitful exercises in the rethinking of historical problems, but here we are concerned with the beginning student who has to be taught to think historically at all. He, it seems to me, needs a framework, an interpretative scheme, of manifest meaning, however much he may ultimately come to progress by rejecting that framework and that interpretation. After all, the teaching and learning of history consist in great part of such iterated breaking-up, but before a thing can be broken up it has first of all to exist.

One of the best 'large' subjects for undergraduate study is the history of political thought. Politics—the problem of political organization and action—must always constitute a large part of any undergraduate history course; to attempt a study of other ways in which society expresses itself, as for instance through art or agriculture, without some understanding of political events and conditions is to encourage only woolliness and pretence. But to go on from what happens in political life to what, over the long ages, great minds have thought and said about it, is to most students a highly illuminating experience. They learn to think on a new plain of abstraction; since they deal with people who often read each other they get a feeling for continuity and interaction; and at the same time they learn to distinguish the permanent from the occasional, the universal from the particular. Probably all well-constructed intellectual history can serve this purpose : one might choose the history of science or of economic thought or of religion. The advantages of political thought are purely practical : it has long been studied and many good books on it exist; it has been exceptionally continuous; it bears directly on a main part of the student's 'hard' history; and it deals with problems which require little specialized or technical knowledge. I should always make it a main subject in any syllabus, especially if it were accompanied by other 'large' subjects more specifically directed to an understanding of what happened rather than what people thought.

The other kind of subject—that which teaches analytical reasoning—must even more obviously have its own coherence. Since, by definition, it will have to be much more restricted in time and space, there is no problem here. The kind of topic to be looked for is one in which at least some primary evidence is available to the undergraduate, and which casts up precise and narrow questions for him to consider. As against the 'large' subject, which preferably should compel a man to consider every aspect of a given age and society, the 'narrow' subject should be 'tunnel history'—should specifically concern itself with, say, the constitutional or economic or military history of one country over a relatively short stretch of time, perhaps a century or two. I prefer constitutional or economic history to such other possibilities as general political history or the history of ideas for three main reasons : because they throw up the more clearly defined problems, because as a rule they contain more solved problems a study of which will show the student how such reasoning is done, and because they involve him in learning some technicalities (the structure of law courts, the power of the executive, price mechanism or the labour market) which force him to think with precision. Of course, I am here concerned entirely with the student who is taught, with a man who must essentially take all his information at second hand. Unlike the student who pursues research of his own, he will find the solved questions much more instructive than the unsolved ones, provided it is understood that in history 'solved' is a relative term : the student should always be kept aware of the dark patches and the debates. In addition, it is necessary that the good teacher should combine the pedagogue's necessary dogmatism with the fellow-scholar's free exchange of ideas, even when dealing with undergraduates.

One kind of subject, growingly popular, seems to me unfortunate. There is an increasing interest in historiography, the study of historians, and there is no doubt that it can be a fascinating study, especially when it is treated properly as a form of the history of ideas. But when, as too often, it becomes only a confrontation of conflicting views, it is not a good way to teach history because it directs the attention away from what happened to what was later said about it. Students are only too ready to absorb and present 'rival views' of a problem rather than come to grips with the problem itself, for the discussion is ready made and easily creates a spurious impression of learned depth. This fashion for discussing historians rather than history helps to destroy any sense, tenuous enough at the best of times in most undergraduates, that what they are reading about actually once happened, actually is life. A special historiographical topic is as legitimate as the study of any form of human thought, but it is also exceptionally difficult, insufficiently explored, and liable to be a little precious. Good historians are not primarily men of ideas, and to make them shoulder the burden of carrying the thought of an age is to overload them; if treated with a sense of proportion, they cannot, in honesty, appear so important or exciting as more theoretical thinkers. Anyhow, the infiltration of historiographical methods into the study of straight historical problems should be kept to a minimum : it leads to a misunderstanding of what history is about and to a false sense of profundity in the student. All those booklets and pamphlets which treat historical problems by collecting extracts from historians writing about them give off a clear light only when a match is put to them.

Subjects of both the types distinguished—wide and narrow—are plentiful, nor, from the point of view of intellectual analysis, does it matter which are selected. In practice, however, it does matter, if only because some choice has to be made. There are certain considerations which can assist in the choice, apart from that most commonly applied, which is established usage. Why should one not simply continue to teach those parts of history traditionally taught in a given university system, provided they offer a sufficient range of both types, since one satisfactory subject is as good as another? Why not, indeed—except for two things. In the first place, fashions change as well as interests, and established subjects can become bores to teachers and taught alike. Since there is no virtue whatever in boredom—only an ass justifies any form of study on the grounds that it is a distasteful discipline and therefore good for the soul— historical subjects can lose their usefulness and should be removed before they rot. Secondly, historians themselves change their approach to old problems often enough to necessitate a change also in the teaching of them, although as a rule such changes can be made without altering the ostensible description. While, for instance, English constitutional history was for long taught as a series of legal issues and problems (an approach which often provided an excellent training in rigorous analysis) it is nowadays regarded much more as one form of 'social' history in which the particular problems of government are related to social structure, personal relationships, and the distribution of wealth. There is here a very real gain in insight and depth, nor need this necessarily be accompanied by the loss of rigour which in practice has often resulted. But the alert teacher, himself a working historian, should be able to re-define the contents of his subject without having to devise a new label, provided the subject is still alive. And nearly all historical subjects are in fact immortal, metamorphosing internally, sometimes out of recognition, while wearing the same suit of clothes to the casual eye.

Still, the search for proper subjects to teach is an unending one, and at the present time, when historians' own interests have everywhere expanded to take in more parts of the world and additional regions of human activity, the pressure to bring in the new just because of its novelty is great. It is a double pressure, for the desires of the teachers in command of novel subjects are matched by the desires of lively young minds to find new things to think about. Neither pressure is always legitimate; we have all met the determined builders of empire and the addicts to frivolous mutability. Yet at heart the arguments are serious and proper: historical studies must renovate themselves not only by filling old bottles with new wine but on occasion also by buying in some new bottles, sometimes unhappily filled with some rather ancient and vinegary stuff. It is therefore to be hoped that in constructing courses of study academic teachers will observe some general rules. If in their search for specific subjects that satisfy the need for narrow and large topics they keep in mind something like absolute criteria, they may hope to avoid the disaster which strikes a school of history when things are thrust in all anyhow, just because someone wants them and has a loud enough voice.[4]

The criteria I wish to put forward may not look

---

[4] Of course, in some universities, especially smaller ones, what is to be taught must depend on the skills of the limited teaching staff available. But in an era of expansion this is a diminishing problem; and in any case, teachers' interests can be directed by the teaching syllabus.

very impressive, but they seem to me exhaustive. They are two pairs of opposites. There are advantages in the familiar and the unfamiliar, and there are advantages in coherence and in variety. If the student is really to learn how to handle evidence, weigh up conflicting views, and analyse problems, it seems unwise to train him on subject matter with which he has no previous acquaintance. Furthermore, all historical understanding involves some grasp of the conventional attitudes and behaviour of another age and, possibly, place. The student has to become aware of how the people he reads about commonly thought and acted, in a manner so obvious to themselves that they rarely made it explicit but far from obvious to other ages and societies. This is a very difficult thing to do, and more difficult in the face of unfamiliar pieces of history. On the other hand, a familiar piece—for instance, a period already studied in some depth at school—will start the undergraduate off a little way ahead of the baseline, so that he will have more time available to learn the practices and benefits of serious study. However, familiar subjects may unquestionably become very tedious. This is particularly true in the English educational system which ensures, through premature specialization, that people anticipate university work in their last two years at school. If on arriving at the university they find themselves faced once more with a topic which they believe themselves to have studied already, they are likely to become frustrated and resentful. There are ways of overcoming this (of which the best one, naturally, is really first-class and exciting teaching) nor is it invariably the case that a student does not want to go more deeply into something that he has already become quite well acquainted with, but no one will deny that the introduction of a new and unfamiliar subject can have the most stimulating effect, provided it is treated in an intellectually respectable fashion.

The rival advantages of coherence and variety are equally difficult to balance. By coherence I mean a scheme in which the various subjects bear upon one another. For instance, the student of ancient political thought might also be required to work on the general history of Greece and Rome; the study of Australian history might be accompanied by work on both the history of British expansion and the problems of the Pacific; the history of England would be read together with the history of Western Europe. A special and specially useful form of coherence is provided by continuity. Since one of the services of history to the human mind consists in enlarging the imagination and understanding through time, in giving a sense of things happening in a rational and interlocking sequence, there is much virtue in a fairly intensive study of one area through long periods. If the study is to be intensive this means not a single large outline but a series of topics taking over from one another: the study of the whole of English history, for instance, might be demanded, divided into three or four manageable sections. On the other hand, such concentration on one region or nation can prove stultifying: it can limit the vision quite unduly and can lead to intellectual lethargy in the student. Therefore the course should include variety, that is subjects not manifestly connected with each other, so as to restimulate interest at intervals, to provide new openings for the mind, and to apply the spur of unexpected comparisons and contrasts. Thus a historical syllabus which includes only political topics, or only topics related to England and Europe, is seriously deficient; one need not fall for the present fashion which seeks salvation from the urban congestion of Britain in the steppes and pampas to believe that no course is well designed unless it provides for the teaching of diverse and unfamiliar bits of history.

The problems posed by these pairs of opposites, all desirable, cannot, in the conditions of a three- or four-year course, be resolved without compromise. In choosing subjects to teach, the teacher will be wise to avoid the visionary and to remember the capacities of the student. I suggest that a good course will provide familiar and coherent topics in order to teach analysis and rigour, while it will seek to train the historical imagination by means of unfamiliar and various subjects. Of course, this does not mean that the former section needs to be devoid of imagination or the latter of rigour. It does mean that the overriding necessity of training the student in both these mental aptitudes will be served most successfully by assigning the chief part in one task to the familiar and coherent subject where concentration in depth becomes possible, and in the other task to a ranging series of less obvious options. The kind of course here advocated would, in fact, consist of a compulsory backbone with a free choice among additional members. The backbone should be composed of a familiar subject studied in depth and designed to train the intellect by means of the study of primary sources, historical controversies, and specific problems. In practice, I suppose, this is likely to mean that a student would have to work on the history of his own country, and despite a good deal of opposition to this principle I cannot see what may be wrong with it. True, excessive insularity and chauvinistic prejudice can lie in wait there, and in the illiberal or aggressive countries of the world such dangers are real. I should probably hesitate to recommend my scheme in Russia or Indonesia, countries where the historian ought to do his best to redress the patriotic balance. But in Britain, the older Commonwealth countries, and up to a point the United States, where most historians (like most intellectuals) are only too likely to regard their own country's history with feelings that range from critical scepticism to blatant cynicism, the danger of producing yet another generation of chauvinists seems pretty remote. On the other hand, when it comes to the training of the reasoning faculty, the advantages provided by a longish period with the main outlines of which the student is familiar, and by the fact that he knows the country and language in question, are so overwhelming that I find the frequent attacks on English history in English schools of history hard to understand; or rather, I should find them hard to understand if I thought that the attackers were pursuing intellectual ends rather than political and social—were concerned to train reasoning intelligences rather than produce supposedly desirable beings—worthy citizens of the world, admirers of the United Nations, or even Friends of the Soviet Union.

The other parts of the scheme will have to take account of what can be taught; new subjects, however striking, must prove that they rely on a sufficient range of serious scholarly work, that neither their problems nor the treatment of them need be trivial, and that the reason for teaching them lies in their ability to stimulate the imaginative and coordinating powers of the trained intelligence. Here some liberty of choice should be given to the student, though experience proves an excessive number of options to be more of a burden than a joy. Advice on this is pointless; circumstances and available talent determine what can be done. For myself I should always like to offer something to the man who wishes to opt for coherence rather than variety, as well as to the other kind of student; I see little advantage in compelling a student to collect a number of detached topics if he does not wish to do so, but also no justification for pushing everybody into the single straitjacket of a narrowly conceived course. The student whose backbone subject is English history can have his imagination trained very well by crossing the Channel; he need not cross the oceans, though I should hope that he would wish to do so, and I would naturally give him the opportunity. The boundaries that he should really be encouraged to cross are of another kind: if his intense study concentrates on the political, economic or social problems of society, he should be guided in his choice of options to range into fields of intellectual history as well.

One thing, however, needs stressing once more. The undergraduate reading history should be taught history, not the medley called inter-disciplinary studies which is increasingly fashionable in reformist circles. Since it is the intention to train his mind, there have to be a specific content and a hard outline to what he is doing. Bits of history mingled with bits of philosophy and literature, taught by different specialists with quite dissimilar intellectual concerns, may seem a good way to provide what is known as a broad education; but in terms of a genuine university experience, it is in fact a bad way. The university must train the mind, not fill the untrained mind with multi-coloured information and undigested ideas, and only the proper study of an identifiable discipline according to the rules and practices of that discipline can accomplish that fundamental purpose. Certainly, teachers of history should concern themselves with their charges' broader education; they should want them to know some poetry and art, have some idea about philosophic or theological concepts, understand a bit of the teaching of economists, lawyers and natural scientists. However, this is nothing to do with the framing of courses for study and examination, with the real work of intellectual training. There is no greater heresy in the teacher than the familiar conviction that students will learn nothing in which they are not examined. Should our thinking really be determined by the student who will never read a poem unless he has to sit a paper in English literature, or even by the eminent scholar (*absit nomen*) who has told us that it took the battle of Stalingrad to open his eyes to the existence of a world and a history beyond the confines of medieval Germany? The historian should regard his subject as capable of training and equipping reasoning intelligences and should use it for that purpose; his concern for the wider interests of a civilized mind he should express in the manner and method of his teaching.

2 Undergraduate Teaching: How?

Teachers and students—especially teachers—differ so widely that it may be quite pointless to offer any personal views on methods of teaching. On this topic, instruction of any kind, however well meant or well disguised, would certainly be resented. If I nevertheless go on to consider these matters, it is because I am convinced that whatever may be done must be controlled by thinking in principle, because I believe that I can offer certain considerations which amount to a principled set of conditions, and because it may be useful to describe from experience how these considerations work out in practice.

In the first place, if history is a subject (as has been argued) in which to teach cannot mean merely to convey information or instruct in techniques but must mean to assist in the formation of a given type of trained mind, it follows that in a sense it cannot be taught at all but only learned. At least—and this is the more accurate as well as less absurd way of putting it—the process of teaching must be quite exceptionally two-way, must involve a most active participation from both workers in the operation. Subjects like law and engineering, the sciences and classics, in which a great deal of factual knowledge and acquired expertise must be transferred to the new practitioner, can and should teach a lot by straightforward instruction. History has just enough of such matters in it—for no one can work on it without some factual knowledge and some mental techniques, such as summarizing and paraphrasing texts or computing and analysing figures—to maintain a solid core of instruction in its teaching, but if there were nothing else it would not even begin to be the teaching subject 'history' that we know. Its main purpose requires something different: a dialogue, sometimes a dispute, in which the superior knowledge and equipment of the teacher calls forth the student's active creation of his own knowledge and equipment.

Before teaching methods are considered, one point needs to be made. It is fundamental to a successful course of study in history that the student should read widely, thoroughly and purposefully for himself. Any teacher who confines his task to what in the jargon of the educational civil service is called 'student-confrontation hours' deserves to have his labours classified in that kind of language. More important: any student who thinks that his time divides between the hours of work when he sits in class and the remainder when he does not—the 'on-parade, off-parade' attitude which is becoming distressingly familiar—had better be rapidly disabused of such nonsense. All this may seem too obvious to need mention, but is it? Administrators refuse to recognize that the teacher is not necessarily dissociated from teaching when he meets students casually, when he reads to keep up with the work of his colleagues, or when he pursues his share in the discovery and display of new knowledge and interpretations. And bitter experience shows that undergraduates increasingly conceive their task in terms of attendance at somebody's formal instruction. Both teaching and learning are full-time, day-long activities, a fact which justifies the rather long breaks in immediate contact conventionally called vacations which in fact are commonly filled with a continuation of the teaching scholar's activities, slightly transformed by the temporary absence of instruction in the limited sense. The student, too, needs to think of vacations as times for a change in his work rather than a cessation from it. These may be counsels of tediously traditional perfection, and university systems with long terms and short vacations no doubt have to find other ways of adjusting the relationship between periods of direct contact and periods of separation, for instance by calling professors into the presence of students only two or three days each week.[5] Nowadays students must also find time to earn the money which, sometimes, is used to see them through college. Yet though practice will always fall short of the ideal, I remain convinced that it would be very wrong to replace the old ideal by a new and more realistic one. At least we must never cease to work towards a situation in which the active labours of teaching and study fill the year and every day of it.[6] And for the student this means

[5] I prefer the system under which I work: very heavy direct teaching duties in short terms, followed by comparatively long periods during which the concentration can shift to reading, research and writing. Or it could if the world were properly organized.

[6] When I was first a research student, my supervisor said to me,

much reading designed by himself and carried out on his own, an activity which results only indirectly from the specific teaching work done by the instructor, but which distinguishes the true student from the counterfeit.

However, we must turn to the ways in which the instructor specifically teaches. I am aware of the many discussions concerning so-called teaching aids and so-called new methods, sometimes involving teaching machines, closed-circuit television, or 'practicals' like undergraduate research projects. In the main, however, these are only variations on traditional methods, intended to adjust the situation to new mass audiences. In the study of history, the printed book remains the best 'teaching aid', and nothing can replace a trained ability to read. Similarly, it may be enterprising to present one expert to more people by means of television, but he is still giving a lecture, though he will be hampered in effect by his lack of physical contact with the class. When all is said, methods of teaching remain traditional, and there are basically three of them; since all three are in use in my university (Cambridge) I have had some experience of them all. They are firstly the lecture in which one teacher addresses a variable group of students, sometimes (but outside the United States very rarely) replying to questions and interjections; secondly the class or seminar, a gathering, preferably round a table, of a group with a presiding teacher in which individual students present views or even papers for guided discussion by the group; and thirdly the meeting of one or at most two students with an instructor in which written work by the student is discussed and criticized (super-

---

quite seriously, at the end of the first term: 'Now don't work every day of the vacations; do take Christmas Day off.' I fear that I took Boxing Day off as well.

vision, tutorial). It is my belief that a good history school will make full use of all three methods because they complement one another; each does something that the others cannot do.

The lecture, possibly, needs defending to-day; some newly founded institutions are trying to do without it. Certainly, as a teaching method it has its dubious side. However, in some places the ancient reliance on teaching by lectures only still prevails, though everywhere in England, at least, teachers are trying to introduce the other methods in which discussion rather than instruction predominates. Oxford cherishes an old-established prejudice against lectures, not unjustified, if reports are true, by the standard of lecturing encountered. On the principle already stated that the teaching of history should rest on a two-way traffic of debate, the replacement of lectures by group or individual supervision must be welcomed. Nevertheless, it seems to me too early to abandon lecturing as a method of teaching, but a great deal depends on the place assigned to the use of lectures. The invention of printing put a term to the lecture's necessary predominance in teaching and at least called for a reassessment of its purposes, though too many university people—students as well as teachers—seem to be unaware of this. The lecturer has no business to attempt that which the book can do better. Thus it is wrong to use the lecture in order to convey information either on facts or arguments which is available in print. The lecture should not 'cover the syllabus', that is to say, supply the student with what he needs to pass examinations. It cannot afford to be dull, inaudible, incomprehensible; it must not yield a set of student's notes reading like the abstract of a textbook.

What, then, can it do? The chief purposes for which it remains uniquely useful are two. In the first place, it can communicate new knowledge not yet found in the books, a function of no little importance but in history not likely to be called frequently into use. More important, it can and must provide the stimulus of a live contact with another intelligence wrestling with the problems of history. This means that the lecturer *must* endeavour to be new, even original, even wild, at all costs. It is his task to bring to the student, especially the not uncommon student reared on books that suggest a kind of complete and finished quality in historical knowledge, a real sense of the fluidity inherent in enquiry, debate, disagreement. Reading books, even reading many books, is always liable to leave the beginner with the impression that history can be learned by absorbing other people's words: the lecturer must shock him out of that state. Of course, he should be lively and vigorous and deeply concerned; why should any listener be interested in what appears to bore the lecturer himself? But this liveliness is by no means to be confined to manner; I am not advocating a mere theatrical playing to the gallery or that search for popularity by such means as blue jokes, contrived paradox, rhetorical device which one sometimes encounters. The life of a lecture should come from its contents, and it comes from them if the student is confronted with new ideas, new interpretations, new associations, new comparisons, if the surprise stems from the unexpectedness of the intellectual attack, not from the decorative dressing. Wit, humour, savagery, even obscenity can all be justified at times, but none for their own sakes; they are only the means to wrest the student out of stupor, uncork his ears, and alert him to the real message, which is that history is never done, and all he has learned needs to be called in doubt, that he himself is a member of a band jointly engaged in trying to disentangle the truth about the past. The lecturer should disseminate a sense of a scholar at work, and he should occasionally demonstrate how that work is done : few things enthral an undergraduate audience more than an exposition of the technicalities of research, provided the dosage is not too large. In general it is less important for a lecturer to be 'right' than to be alive—alive as a working scholar—for it is his function to cast doubt upon the possibility that in historical studies anyone will ever be finally 'right'. The necessary redressing of the scepticism so engendered can be left to the other occasions of teaching; let the lecturer stick to the task of destroying overfamiliar landmarks and boundaries, of building new structures to be tested by the student, of removing the school-produced, book-confirmed shell of acquisitive learning which can guard the critical faculty like a carapace.

Therefore the best lecture courses are quite brief, perhaps some twelve to fifteen lectures long. The matter to be handled does not affect the issue; if a lecturer is required to cover really long periods of history in detail, he is being asked to do the wrong thing, to take the place of books, but he can and should contribute also to the study of large and long subjects. Thus suppose a university offers a course on Europe since the Renaissance, a common enough thing. To ask any lecturer, or even several in sequence, to utter comprehensively on this sprawling monstrosity of a subject from the rostrum is quite absurd, which does not at all mean that the course itself is absurd. Some forty or more lectures on such a subject, going steadily through the years and countries, can serve no purpose except to supplant the printed book. On the other hand, three or four sets of ten lectures each, taking a section or a topic, tearing it apart and building it up again, organized around a theme and determined to shake if not to shock, can restore meaning and excitement to what at first may well appear to be a worn-out subject. Lectures should be arranged either to do this for the large and familiar subjects, or else they should be used to treat of some (unpublished) specialist matter; in either case, quite short runs will do much better than weeks on end plodding through time.

There is no need to discuss the technical skills required. No two people lecture alike: at least, none should, for in a lecture a man must stand forth, must impose and display himself. He will naturally avoid the obvious faults: he will not read a script, mumble to himself, address a blackboard or some high corner in the far end of the room, walk about too much. He must establish contact with the audience, which means that he must physically and visibly address them, be constantly aware of them (for instance, catch their yawns), and be careful of the tedium promoted by too even and unmodulated a delivery. For the rest, whether he speaks fast or slowly, uses notes or none, constructs a work of art or runs off at the mouth, it will be up to him to choose what suits him best. Provided he keeps before him the duty of doing what the printed page cannot do, he will do well.

It may be argued that this task of disturbing set notions and stimulating the student's interest is better performed by methods which rely on discussion rather than discourse. Though, of course, all teaching of history will seek to some extent to call forth new thinking, the lecture has advantages of its own. For one thing it is economical. The lecturer can get at scores or hundreds of students at a time, and since the sort of lecture here described must be given by experts still at work in the labour of discovering historical truth, much is gained by enabling all students to hear them. For another, a lecturer can take risks not open to the man conducting a discussion group. He need not feel obliged to stand by every word he says, he can be rash, he can be flippant, he can be passionately serious, all attitudes which sound quite false in the intimacy of a seminar but often work efficiently from the platform. Above all, some people just are good at lecturing and not so good at handling a discussion. Of course, if the lecturer is good at answering impromptu questions he can add this to his technique, though if he does he must always remember one golden rule: be as sharp as you like about books and scholars and even history, but never show the faintest trace of contempt for or impatience with your audience.[7] The question may be stupid: it must still be treated with total seriousness. Of course, if it is malicious the case is altered. The student who refuses to accept that the process before him is a joint enterprise deserves the hard answer.

The other methods of teaching history are generally accepted as good and need no defence. On the other hand, it may be useful to distinguish between them, for the seminar and tutorial differ in more than size. The class or seminar should provide a genuine discussion among the students themselves, neither a lecture from the chair nor a dialogue between the teacher and one undergraduate. Everybody must be involved, though to achieve this is one of the most difficult tasks for the teacher who has to combine some of the qualities required in the conductor of an orchestra, Speaker of the House of Commons, and lion-tamer. Although it will be necessary to assign specific tasks to individuals—to appoint probably two 'reporters' on an assigned theme—

---

[7] This applies to all teaching. Sarcasm is out.

the rest of the class must on all accounts be prevented from just listening or possibly going to sleep, or doing a crossword puzzle. This means that, as a rule, the topics to be discussed cannot be too particular and narrow, or at least that they must be of the kind that is central to the whole historical subject being studied by the class. Thus everybody will feel stirred to come in. Ideally, an undergraduate class should have some of the feeling of the graduate seminar, which is to say that the participants should have a sense of sharing in the discovery of historical truth. In practice this makes for some difficulties well worth watching out for. It is quite unlikely that an undergraduate class will in fact be operating on the frontiers of knowledge, nor is it particularly desirable that they should. As the teacher will probably be taking the same sort of class year by year he will become excessively familiar with all the poss-ibilities contained in the material and the limits set by undergraduates' knowledge and experience. The tempta-tion to replace discussion and search by instruction and information increases every year. On the other hand, the students are necessarily aware that their class debates things often debated before; given half a chance, many of them will seek the short-cut of receiving a lecture. Keeping a class at its proper level of multiple discussion tests the teacher severely, but the rewards are worth the labour. No other method so readily produces a development of ideas, a working out of problems, and a genuine interaction among several minds. A good class probably gives the student the clearest idea of what the study of history is about.

Lastly, the individual supervision or tutorial, or if not individual then at least never larger than two students with one teacher. This is the special pride of the old universities of England, and it certainly can be a most effective way of teaching. Of course, it is immensely uneconomical; a teacher charged with ten students will have to go over the same ground five or ten times. When the student is silent, very slow, or idle the tutorial can be sheer pointless agony; and if the teacher becomes bored or indifferent—a danger greater in this method than any other—the purpose of the whole operation collapses. This can happen especially if the teacher does too much of this kind of work; the normal maximum of twelve hours a week permitted at Cambridge is probably already too high, and the horror stories coming from Oxford, where, one hears, tutors are likely to be doing twenty hours or more, testify to an imbalance in the teaching system.[8] But the good supervision deserves the praise given to it. Its essence consists in the analysis and consideration of a specific circumscribed topic in a dialogue between teacher and pupil. No doubt the customary essay, written by the pupil on a subject given to him (with a reading list) by the teacher, forms the best foundation for this. It compels the student not only to study a problem but to understand it and formulate his own answer; it enables the teacher to guide the student's mind into proper attitudes of analytical rigour, comprehension in depth, and adequate expression. In other words, he teaches him to think and react like an historian, and (hopefully) to write like a good historian. By its intimacy and intensity the super-

[8] There is also the question of how many supervisions a student should have; at Cambridge, some scientists undergo up to four a week. Such practices are bound to turn the supervision hour into a period of mere instruction, concerned perhaps with the solving of set problems with finite answers, a method which may be suitable in some subjects and is widely practised in the teaching of law, too. In history it is out of place, and one supervision a week is probably right, even if this means that many issues are left undiscussed.

vision creates, at its best, a genuine scholarly link between the partners in the enterprise, but even when it falls short of that (as commonly it does) it is bound to elevate the student above the role of mere receptacle. Since he has had to do real productive work, the vital element of his active share is secured.

Trouble arises if the supervision is used to do the work properly performed by one of the other methods. One hears of tutors who employ their time to replace lectures or even to 'cover the ground', that is to replace private reading. Any useful discussion of the student's essay will naturally range beyond its particular problem, though this must be clarified first, but that is not the same thing as giving general instruction. More insidiously, quite a few people seem to think that the class can take the place of supervisions and should do so. They argue that the class is less wasteful of man-hours, and that a class held by an expert will profit the student more than supervisions by a man who of necessity cannot be expert in everything he has to teach. But cogent as such arguments are, they overlook a difference in functions and potential. I do not think that the supervision can do the work of the class in starting genuine debates and cooperative enquiry; but neither can the class give that sense of sitting together with a trained mind and actively interested teacher, concerned (for the moment) only with oneself. It is also possible to get away with things in a class—with imprecise thinking, slipshod expression, bad writing, and an unconscious lack of understanding—which the direct and relentless questioning of the supervision exposes and corrects. Quite possibly, among the three methods described the tutorial may be thought the 'best', but I see no virtue in such hierarchies. By itself the tutorial is no more sufficient or satisfactory than any other method. Each contributes its own special gifts to the tasks of teaching and study; each can be used well or badly; between them they are capable of training minds to a clear understanding of problems, a right use of reason, a passion for intellectual exercise, and an ability to frame answers in convincing ways.

I do not propose to touch on the question of examinations. Methods differ widely, from the constant grading common at most American institutions, to the once-for-all ordeal, after three years' work, of the University of London. I like none of them particularly well, but I recognize the necessity for something of the kind. At any rate, the three methods of teaching history here described will work within any arrangement of syllabus or examination. The student who has passed actively through a course using all of them in competent hands, and who in addition has found his way to the library, will know at the end why he came to university to read history.

3 The Graduate Student

The graduate student needs teaching very different from that given to the undergraduate; it would be a serious mistake to suppose—though a mistake which I think is quite often made—that he is merely a somewhat enlarged version of his earlier identity. Should he, indeed, be taught at all, in the sense that the undergraduate unquestionably is?

It must be said that this question can probably be asked only in England, the only country known to me where a happy, gentlemanly, even dilettante attitude can still be found here and there in the universities, where B.A.s sometimes think that they have learned all they need to know, and where research students are still too frequently left to their own devices. One still meets dons who hold that a man who cannot make the grade (that is, obtain the Ph.D. degree) on his own is not cut out for a scholar's career. On the other hand, I once met a student who in a discussion of training courses declared that the research student's inviolate soul rejected all such things as interference—though admittedly he was a New Zealander.[9] At the other end of the scale we find the American graduate school, with its schematized demands of general study and 'comprehensive' examinations in varied subjects, a system in which the dissertation, so vital in England, almost takes second place. I will say at once that I take my stand somewhere between these extremes, believing that graduate students are indeed students and therefore should be taught, but that their work should be very definitely, even excessively, concentrated upon the specialist study they have undertaken. If these issues are to be raised above the level of personal taste, it becomes again necessary to ask precisely what purpose those years spent in graduate study are meant to serve.

While one does well, as I have said, to treat the undergraduate as though he were a future scholar even though only a very few ever will be, the graduate student has no end in mind except to equip himself for a career of scholarship. His life is that of an apprentice learning a craft, and his dissertation represents proof of his claim to have learned that craft, to have become fit for membership of a profession.[10] And the profession is that

[9] He is now an eminent professor, and I wonder if he has changed his opinion. It has to be conceded that he made himself into a very fine scholar, without courses of instruction and with not too much assistance.

[10] There is therefore much to be said for what is usually a gibe: the Ph.D. *is* a union card because it proves the owner to have been fully trained. Or rather, that is what it ought to prove.

of the working scholar rather than of the teacher; despite some rather desperate attempts here and there, no one has yet succeeded in training academic historians as teachers, and that accomplishment is left to be acquired by natural aptitude, imitation of exemplars, and experience. I am not myself persuaded that this is a bad thing, or that formal teacher-training courses would be profitable. But the craftsmanship of historical scholarship can be tested, and therefore it can and should be taught. The young man who has obtained his doctorate has proved only one thing: that he has the basic equipment to pursue a life of scholarship. He may claim credence for his work because he has convinced experienced elders that he has absorbed the canons of rational research and controlled judgment. Whether he is an historian, or what sort of an historian he may be, he will, one hopes, go on to show thereafter. His dissertation is not, or should not be, the same thing as the books he will presumably go on to write, any more than the tool-chest made by the apprentice carpenter for his masterpiece represents the norm of his later production.[11]

The teaching of research students must therefore concentrate on the competences which a newly fledged historian is supposed to possess. I suggest that these are: a thorough knowledge of the materials, primary and secondary, available for the study of his chosen area of operations; ability to use these materials, both in the sense of discovering and understanding them, and in the sense of being able to evaluate them critically; ability to formulate meaningful questions and relevant answers; ability to present a sound reconstruction of a

[11] A masterpiece, in defiance of the usual metaphorical usage, originally meant something that lay at the foundation of a man's life's work; it did not crown it.

piece of history, founded with painful accuracy on the evidence; ability to present this reconstruction according to the conventions of historical writing, as for instance in the proper drafting of footnotes and references. I do not believe that at this stage of his career he should be required to prove a wide knowledge of history in general or a superior ability to write on the grand scale. These are skills that come with further learning and experience; a technically competent standard of scholarship is a sufficiently demanding test for the apprentice; and in any case, it is the craftsmanship rather than the art which the young historian must learn first and must prove himself possessed of if he is to be taken seriously as a scholar.

Therefore the form of instruction follows naturally from these ends in view. It is wrong to subject the graduate student to further courses of general history at second hand. Of course, in order to produce a worthy specialist study he needs to have a sufficiently general knowledge of his chosen area, and whether he should be made to study this further depends on the standard of knowledge he has attained with his first degree. This standard differs in different university systems, and I concede that most American or Australian bachelors of arts need to do some more work of the type associated in England with undergraduate studies before they are ready to embark on research.[12] Nothing, however, it seems to me, justifies the imposition of further study outside a man's chosen field. Concentration on the one task in hand, the bane of undergraduate studies, is the

---

[12] This is not intended as an insult. The English B.A. usually lacks the breadth and variety of knowledge (especially of languages) that distinguish his American and Australian counterparts, but his previous experience happens to have fitted him more completely for the one further purpose of research.

only proper attitude for the research student. If he wants to work in Tudor history, he should have a good working knowledge of England in the sixteenth century; he need not, at this stage, be required to show a knowledge of sixteenth-century France or Renaissance culture; and he must not be troubled with any other more distant bits of ancient, medieval or modern history, as he is in some American graduate schools. His labours are determined by the one consideration that he is training himself in the craftsmanship of history by means of the one successful method known, the practical method of writing an original piece of work.

The teaching for this purpose falls naturally into three stages, more or less consecutive though there may be overlaps. At the introductory stage, the student needs to be equipped with the technical skills required of him. He must be taught to survey the area of his concerns and its material, guided to the bibliographical and archival aids, made to learn any languages likely to be encountered in the work, taught to read the handwriting of his manuscripts (supposing it represents a problem), and led to a proper understanding of their meaning. He is thus given the foundations of scholarship in the abstract, as it were, though of course the solidity of these foundations depends on the manner in which he renders them concrete by his own labours in research. These matters can be taught in classes, by a mixture of lectures and discussion, though this depends on there being enough students with allied interests to arrange group teaching. If there are not, the individual teacher must see to it that his individual student receives this instruction. If the skills required are technical in the narrow sense—for example, medieval palaeography, statistics, economic theory—proper organized courses should be available, and the student should preferably be compelled to attend them—perhaps even face examinations in them. Two or three months of this kind of instruction (the student's first term) should ordinarily suffice, but much time is saved, heartbreak averted, and certainty created if this stage of the training is as systematic and organized as possible.

Having laid such technical foundations and roughly defined his proper subject, the student will now start on the research itself. That is to say, he will begin to study his potential material and attempt to ask useful questions of it. The sooner he gets to this stage the better; months spent in generalized preparation sound all very fine and systematic, but in practice they prove disheartening. It is important that the research student should quickly grasp how very different his existence and concerns are from those of the undergraduate, how more intensive and continuous his labours, how more precise and narrow his interests. I like to send my students to their sources within four weeks of arrival, and the longer one waits the harder it becomes to change the undergraduate into the graduate student. From the moment that he begins to read his sources, the student is in some ways on his own. He can learn his craft only by practising it himself, and, in addition, he is about to become the world's leading expert on some small part of history. However, his being on his own does not mean that he can or should be left to himself. The serious business of teaching the graduate student really begins when the stage of formal or organizable courses is over. The teacher must now devote himself to instilling in his pupil the right methods of research, right standards of criticism, ability to see points and connections—in short to helping him become a working scholar. I know no better way of doing this than the individual supervision. If the teacher has to guide a sufficiently large number of students he may well organize them in a seminar, but he should still see them individually to discuss their work, answer their questions, criticize their deductions, argue their views, and keep abreast of their scholarly development. Such supervision should be regular; the custom sometimes current in England by which the teacher leaves it to the student to ask for a meeting when he thinks he needs one is at this stage unfortunate. How frequent these meetings are depends on individual men and the kind of work they are doing; some may need to bring particular problems of the evidence at frequent intervals, while others may take weeks of solid work to accumulate enough matter to make a discussion with their supervisor fruitful. However, for myself I do not like to allow more than three weeks between supervisions, at least in the first two years of research (and excepting the summer vacations).

The usefulness of the seminar as an instrument of graduate teaching depends on the particular meaning given to this protean concept. In its original form, in nineteenth-century Germany, the seminar consisted of a group of students, working under the direction of one man on a variety of closely allied topics, usually assigned by the professor. Such a seminar takes research problems shared by the group and discusses them round a table, in common. It is probably the best kind of training school ever devised for the scholar, but it has disadvantages. In particular, it constricts choice of subjects and interest, can inhibit new lines of enquiry, and—since the best teachers tend to be the most formidable personalities—is liable to produce disciples rather than fellow-scholars. In any case it cannot exist unless there are at least six or eight men whose subjects of study touch or overlap. If one is faced with a group of students working in roughly the same area but not able to tackle single problems jointly, one may still organize a seminar at which individuals present problems or conclusions arising from their own work for discussion and criticism by the rest, under the teacher's guidance. This is valuable to all concerned, but it is much less like teaching and must not take the place of the individual supervision. I have known seminars which were more like multiple supervision, and I do not think them very useful. Going round the table and asking students briefly to put their questions or state their problems may cut down the labours of supervising, but it is an inefficient and insufficient form of teaching. The German seminar, in its own peculiar circumstances, can cover most of the teaching needed, though even in that system individual confrontation of teacher and student is very desirable. Individual teaching really comes first, to be supplemented by group meetings if they are feasible and so organized as to meet the needs of any given set of people. I do not think that there is an ideal form of seminar; it is a flexible method, adaptable to circumstances, though some forms of it (in which no effective teaching takes place or the teacher is really seeking assistance in his own work) are plainly unsatisfactory.

The third and last stage of the training begins when the student turns to write up his findings. I have known professors who would read no part of a man's dissertation until he had submitted it for examination, on the grounds that the work was to be his, not theirs; and I have known others who regarded the reading and criticizing of written work as practically their sole teaching duty. Both attitudes seem to me rather needlessly extreme. If the student has been thoroughly and properly trained during his researches, it is probable that he will prove competent enough in the use of his material, but the actual task of putting in order a lot of detail and argument is not one that can be learned by instinct. At this point the student needs quite a lot of help in thinking out the scheme of his dissertation, and he should receive every necessary criticism of the product. At the same time, it would be wrong for the teacher to write the dissertation himself, in any sense. Supervisions will probably become fewer at this stage; on the other hand, every time there is a piece of writing in hand it should be gone over thoroughly from the point of view of both content and style. The task of teaching now becomes concrete : the student at last comes to understand fully what may be required of him. But if he was worth admitting in the first place and has since then been properly supervised, he ought to have the ability and equipment which now entitle him to opinions of his own; the teacher must be more careful than before not to impose himself but to act the part of an older colleague whose advice has been asked.

Of course, this description of the various tasks involved in teaching and training graduate students embodies simply a personal experience and a personal attitude. I am very far from claiming universal validity for it, though I admit to thinking it the right way for myself to go about things. It will be seen that I put a lot of weight on teaching, that in my view the supervisor of research students should work very hard. Others may well regard this as too much like direction and even intrusion; some men of experience argue that the teacher should confine himself to guidance and suggestion. But if the practice of history requires aptitudes that can be learned (as well, of course, as aptitudes that are born in the man) then they should surely be taught consciously and with determination. What point is there in leaving such training to chance? Of course, the intensive teaching here advocated has its dangers. One must beware of creating anything like a master-disciple relationship: the student must be kept aware both of his own liberty and of his duty to think and work for himself. It is a good idea to encourage one's students to learn from each other, and an even better one to make them consult other scholars. However much it may please the ego to preside over a 'school' or to dispose of the futures of clever young men, such temptations are really wicked. There is no sadder sight than the young man who knows that all his prospects of a career are bound up with one man's good favour; such things are bad for the character of both teacher and student. The point does not need elaboration; it needs brief mention only because the situation occurs more often than is comfortable to contemplate.

But while this abuse of a teacher's place and duty may lie in wait for the unwary or conceited, it remains true that it must not be avoided by running away from the duty to teach the apprentice historian. Even more than the undergraduate he must be instructed, guided, and trained. In teaching research students, we prepare the next generation of scholars, and this is responsible work, perhaps the most responsible we have, not to be skimped. If we honestly think that the study of history is a proper pursuit for civilized man, that it amounts to a sincere and intense search for the truth, then we must take seriously the task of maintaining this study and this search in future generations. In the end, all depends on what we pass on to others.

Index of Historians

Some Modern Classics in Fontana